Designing Efficient BPM Applications
A Process-Based Guide for Beginners

Christine McKinty and Antoine Mottier

Beijing · Boston · Farnham · Sebastopol · Tokyo

Designing Efficient BPM Applications

by Christine McKinty and Antoine Mottier

Copyright © 2016 Christine McKinty and Antoine Mottier. All rights reserved.

Printed in the United States of America.

Published by O'Reilly Media, Inc., 1005 Gravenstein Highway North, Sebastopol, CA 95472.

O'Reilly books may be purchased for educational, business, or sales promotional use. Online editions are also available for most titles (*http://safaribooksonline.com*). For more information, contact our corporate/institutional sales department: 800-998-9938 or corporate@oreilly.com.

Editor: Brian Foster	**Indexer:** Judy McConville
Production Editor: Nicole Shelby	**Interior Designer:** Monica Kamsvaag
Copyeditor: Kim Cofer	**Cover Designer:** Randy Comer
Proofreader: James Fraleigh	**Illustrator:** Rebecca Demarest

March 2016:   First Edition

Revision History for the First Edition
2016-03-03:   First Release

See *http://oreilly.com/catalog/errata.csp?isbn=9781491924716* for release details.

978-1-491-92471-6

[LSI]

For S,

With much love,

C.
xx

Table of Contents

Preface

Every business uses business processes. These are the everyday tasks you do to obtain and keep customers, maintain a competitive edge, and stay profitable. They are also the tasks that keep the lights on, the coffee machine filled, your phones connected, your payroll run, and your bills sent. This book takes an example that is familiar to all businesses, and shows how you can automate it and turn it into a process-based application. The step-by-step approach, with hands-on examples, leads you through the creation of an online process that is easy to use. With an efficient and repeatable process, you save time and money so you can concentrate on what your business is really about.

Audience

You are a business analyst who is looking for efficiency gains for your business. You have skills in designing workflows and understanding human interactions with processes. You do not necessarily have programming skills, but you know the kind of things that a programmer can do. Where a script or program is needed, the book contains an example that you can copy.

How to Use This Book

The book is a step-by-step guide to creating a process-based application, and each chapter builds on earlier chapters. Read the chapters in order. In each chapter, follow the instructions to develop your application.

First you will create a prototype of the application page using some dummy data. Then you will create the most frequent use flow in a process, and define the data model. After using some temporary forms to check that the basic flow is correct, you will create the real process forms, and then build the first version of the application. The next step will be to add the less frequent process flows into the application, and then connect the application to external information systems. Finally, you will build and test the complete application.

Using Code Examples

Supplemental material (code examples, sample solutions, etc.) is available for download at *https://github.com/oreillymedia/Designing_Efficient_BPM_Applications*.

This book is here to help you get your job done. In general, if example code is offered with this book, you may use it in your programs and documentation. You do not need to contact us for permission unless you're reproducing a significant portion of the code. For example, writing a program that uses several chunks of code from this book does not require permission. Selling or distributing a CD-ROM of examples from O'Reilly books does require permission. Answering a question by citing this book and quoting example code does not require permission. Incorporating a significant amount of example code from this book into your product's documentation does require permission.

We appreciate, but do not require, attribution. An attribution usually includes the title, author, publisher, and ISBN. For example: "*Designing Efficient BPM Applications* by Christine McKinty and Antoine Mottier (O'Reilly). Copyright 2016 Christine McKinty and Antoine Mottier, 978-1-491-92471-6."

If you feel your use of code examples falls outside fair use or the permission given above, feel free to contact us at *permissions@oreilly.com*.

Conventions Used in This Book

The following typographical conventions are used in this book:

Plain text
> Indicates menu titles, menu options, menu buttons, and keyboard accelerators (such as Alt and Control).

Italic
> Indicates new terms, URLs, email addresses, pathnames, filenames, and file extensions.

`Constant width`
> Used for program listings, as well as within paragraphs to refer to program elements such as variable or function names, databases, data types, environment variables, statements, and keywords.

`Constant width bold`
> Shows commands or other text that should be typed literally by the user.

`Constant width italic`
> Shows text that should be replaced with user-supplied values or by values determined by context.

Acknowledgments

Antoine would like to thank Chris, who put in tremendous effort to make this book happen. She initiated the project, defined the structure and authored large parts of the content. Most of all, she is an amazing person to work with!

There are two names on the cover of this book, but thanks are due to many other people without whom this book would never have made it to publication. The authors would like to thank:

- Mickey for encouraging us to go for it and for her help with input to the Introduction.
- Nathalie for her suggestions on how to improve the application page usability.
- Duy and Christophe for testing the application and the instructions for creating it.
- Nico T for his help with graphics.
- Nico C for his awesome review comments.
- Miguel, Charles, and all the Bonitasofters past and present who develop, test, sell, and support Bonita BPM.
- Finally, the customers, consultants, and community users who implement BPMN applications and give us feedback.

May you all continue to have fun!

CHAPTER 1

Recognizing Your Business Processes

> ### Monday Morning
>
> "What d'you mean there's no coffee? This place runs on coffee!"
>
> "We ran out."
>
> "But I told you last week the stock was low. Did we forget to send the order?"
>
> "I sent the order, but someone forgot to pay the previous bill. They won't deliver until it's settled. The person I spoke to was quite brusque...maybe they hadn't had coffee either..."

Maybe your business does not run on coffee, but it certainly runs on something. Whether it's parts for manufacturing, information, or simply money, if your processes are not efficient, you either need to keep a large surplus or risk running out.

This book is all about designing efficient business process applications. The first step is understanding what your business processes are. This chapter defines what a business process is, introduces the Business Process Model and Notation standard, and presents some examples of typical business processes. At the end of the chapter, you will be able to recognize the business processes that you use in your organization.

What Is a Business Process?

A process is a sequence of tasks. Every task is an action, and is carried out by a person or by some automatic system. All processes share certain characteristics:

Interaction over time
> A chronological relationship between tasks, with due dates and sequencing, but not a schedule.

Multiple actors
> More than one person or automatic system must complete tasks for the whole process to be successful.

Repetition
> The sequence of tasks is repeated, either at fixed intervals or when triggered by a specific event.

A process-based application is composed of at least one process and some associated components.

What Is Not a Process?

The action of filling out a form is not a process. A form that has many pages and is filled out online is a single task for a single user. A form that can be filled out in more than one sitting is a single task for a single user. Even a form that has smart fields that depend on other fields, with conditional display, is a single task for a single user.

A state diagram is not a process. A process is constructed from actions. The things that are updated by these actions might have states associated with them, so you might create state diagrams as part of your process validation, but the state diagram is not itself a process.

A business application is not a process. In fact, most business applications contain several related processes, together with some other components. The next section describes some examples of process-based business applications.

Examples of Process-Based Applications

The following examples are familiar to most organizations.

Vacation Management

An employee asks a manager to approve a request to take some days of paid vacation. The manager approves or refuses the request. The employee needs to know how many vacation days are unbooked, and the manager needs to know the vacation plans of the team. Vacation plans change, so requests can also be modified or cancelled.

This is the example that will be used in the rest of this book to guide you through creating a process-based application.

Recruitment and Onboarding

A manager gets permission to recruit, and gives the profile to HR. An HR administrator filters candidates according to the profile, then sends short-listed candidates' details to the manager for review. The manager chooses which candidates to call for an interview. There are selection interviews. A decision is made, and an offer is sent to the selected candidate, who accepts or declines the position. If the candidate accepts, a start date is agreed upon, and the onboarding process is triggered. During the onboarding process, IT creates the user account, Facilities orders an access card for the building and confirms that an office is prepared, HR prepares a welcome pack, and the manager confirms that a ramp-up plan is prepared.

Procure to Pay

An employee raises a purchase order (PO) for new equipment. The employee's manager reviews the purchase order, and approves it or refuses it. If it is above a given validation limit, it is automatically escalated to a senior manager for a second level of approval. After the PO is approved, it is sent to the purchasing department, which places the order. When the equipment is received, it goes to the employee, who checks that it is correct. The invoice is received by Purchasing, which checks that it is correct and initiates payment.

Build to Order

An automated production system receives an order. It checks whether the components needed are in stock, reserves those that are, and orders any that are not. The order is put on hold until the components are all available. When the ordered components arrive at the warehouse, the order is built, then packaged, and then shipped.

Online Shopping

A user logs in to an online shopping site. Over the course of several visits, they assemble a shopping basket. Then they go to the checkout, review the basket content, and select the items for immediate purchase. They check the shipping cost for the selected items. After making a final selection of items to buy, they enter the delivery address and credit card details, which completes the purchase. In the warehouse, a robot collects the purchased items, packages them, and dispatches the order.

Business Continuity

A building surveillance system detects a power outage. It notifies the business continuity (BC) manager at the headquarters of a company with offices in the building. The arrival of the notification automatically starts a timer set for 15 minutes. If the power is still out after 15 minutes, the failover plans are put on standby. The BC manager investigates the cause and decides to declare an incident. This initiates the tracking process, which contacts the staff at the remote site. The managers in the BC team use the process to report their actions, and the process issues reminders or escalations if needed. The BC manager and the whole team can view the process status to get a snapshot of the actions that have been taken. All actions are under the control of the relevant person, while the process provides tracking and visibility for everyone. When the incident is over, a similar tracking process is used to manage the transition back to normal operation.

Document Approval

A technical writer issues a first draft for review. The technical experts review the draft and provide comments in a form. All reviewers can see all comments, which makes it easier to resolve conflicts. The writer produces drafts iteratively, and experts review until they approve the content. The final draft is then sent for proofreading, updated if necessary, then published.

Travel Management

An employee sends a travel request to the team manager. The manager gives provisional approval. The employee sends the travel request to the team administrator, who investigates flight and hotel pricing and availability, and suggests an itinerary. The employee reviews the itinerary, and works with the admin to finalize it. The final itinerary including pricing is sent to the manager, who approves the total cost. The admin books the travel. After the trip, the employee submits an expense claim, which is automatically checked against the expenses policy. If it is in policy, the claim is sent to the finance department for payment. If it is out of policy, it is first sent to the manager for approval of the exceptions and then sent to the finance department for payment.

Business Process Management

Business Process Management (BPM) is an approach to process improvement, like its predecessors Total Quality Management and Continuous Improvement. It is also a technology. Both are focused on improving the efficiency of a business by making processes more efficient, flexible, and dependable, and by reducing costs.

Business Process Model and Notation

Business Process Model and Notation (BPMN) is an international Object Management Group specification for describing a business process. The most recent version is BPMN2. It provides a framework that can be used to define a process so that it can be executed. The standard covers both the graphical representation of a process and the execution semantics. The graphical representation is the basis for communication between the business analysts who design the process and the development team who implement it. It is also useful for communication between the business analysts and the functional teams who are "customers" for the process.

There are BPMN software applications that can take the process definition and create an executable application directly from it. This enables a business process to be presented to nontechnical users in a way that is easy for them to use, efficient, and repeatable. It is therefore much easier to introduce "best practice" and improvements in workflow.

Process Automation

The first step in automating a process is to create a formal definition in BPMN2. This definition can be executed so, at a very basic level, your process is automated.

To transform a process defined in BPMN2 into a process-based application, you need to combine the following:

- Application components that are not part of a process; notably the user interface components, which are typically web pages
- The definitions of all the related processes
- Forms for process tasks that require human interaction
- Data

There is an upfront investment in automating a process, so even if the downstream cost savings are obvious, you will not automate all your processes immediately—or ever. To get the greatest benefit from automation, you should automate a process if it has some of the following characteristics:

- Frequent use
- Approval tasks
- Multiple concurrent use
- Nonhuman tasks that currently require human supervision or intervention
- Strong need for consistency and measurement
- Criticality (for example, time, legislation, or financial risk)

Process Efficiency

The key to creating an efficient process is to start with the simplest case and extend or refine the application iteratively. You can start by automating a small part of the process, and then extend the implementation to cover the whole process, or you can start with a process containing vague or generic tasks and refine it to be more specific based on user feedback.

Summary

Now that you can recognize the business processes you already use, you can make decisions about where to invest in automation and improvements. The rest of this book takes an example that is familiar to all businesses, and shows you step-by-step how to automate it and turn it into a process-based application.

CHAPTER 2

Preparing Your System

In the previous chapter, you learned to recognize the business processes that you use in your company, and how to assess those processes that would most benefit from being automated.

In the rest of the book, you will create an application for managing paid vacation, which includes several processes. This is a typical example: almost every company needs a process for managing paid vacation. This chapter introduces the application by presenting the requirements. It then explains how to install and start the software that you will use to create the application.

Example Application: Vacation Management

Helen Kelly is the HR manager for the ACME corporation, which is a small organization in the business of being an example for BPM process developers. She wants an application that employees can use to track their paid vacation allowance and request days off. The following sidebar contains her description of what she wants.

Vacation Management Application Requirements

Until now, we have managed vacation requests in email and by updating spreadsheets. It's painful for HR and for employees, so we want a tool that will be easy for everyone to use. Something with a cool name so everyone remembers it! It's a tool for employees, managers, and HR. I'm all three, so this is what I want:

As an employee, when I log in to the application, I want it to display the number of days I have available to book and my existing vacation requests. This is a kind of "vacation statement," like a bank statement but for my vacation days! From this page, I want to click a button and fill in a form to request vacation. The request is sent to my manager, who reviews it and approves or refuses it. I also want to be able to

---

change a pending request, or cancel a request. If I ask to cancel an approved request, this should be sent to my manager for review.

As a manager, when I get a request to review, I need to be able to check at a glance that the requester is using up vacation sensibly so that there isn't a big backlog at the end of the year. I need some kind of a vacation statement for the whole team, just available to the manager.

I need approved vacation to be added automatically to the team calendar, so that the whole team can see at a glance who is in work on any date. It would be useful if requested vacation could be in the calendar too, but marked as provisional. That way when I review a request, I can check that there are not too many people absent at the same time.

As HR manager, I need a way to check refusals in case an employee complains that a refusal was unfair. We had a problem last year with one of the teams when the manager refused a lot of vacation requests. The problem was resolved but it made us realize we didn't have good records. We need some kind of tracking of refused requests with the reason for the refusal.

This book uses the vacation management application as an example to illustrate how to create a BPM-based application. If you follow along and develop your application as you read, at the end of the book you will have a working application that you can put into production in your company with just some configuration changes.

The process that is at the heart of the application is the sequence of steps triggered when an employee submits a vacation request, shown in Figure 2-1.

The first step in creating the application is to model this sequence in a BPMN process diagram. To do that, you need to download and install some software, as described in the next sections.

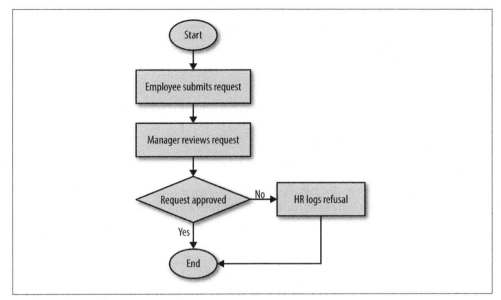

Figure 2-1. Simple vacation request process

Downloads

There are some components to download (*https://github.com/oreillymedia/Design ing_Efficient_BPM_Applications*) that will help you in creating and testing your application:

- *rest-api-extension.zip*, which you will need to create your application home page.
- *Example-InitiateVacationAvailable-1.0.bos*, which initializes the data used in your application.
- *Example-RemoveAllBusinessData-1.0.bos*, which deletes all the data created when you run your application. It can be useful for testing.

There are also some example processes and an application page created following the steps described in this book:

- *Example-NewVacationRequest-1.0.bos*
- *Example-ModifyPendingVacationRequest-1.0.bos*
- *Example-CancelVacationRequest-1.0.bos*
- *page-ExampleVacationManagement.zip*

You also need to download and install some open source software, as described in the next section.

Installing Bonita BPM Community Edition

Throughout the rest of this book, you will see how to create the example application using the Bonita BPM Community Edition software. This is an open source solution for creating and running business process applications.

Download and install the development environment, Bonita BPM Studio. This requires Java 7 or 8 (32- or 64-bits). If you do not already have a suitable Java version, the installer will automatically install it.

Follow these instructions:

1. Go to the Bonitasoft download page (*http://www.bonitasoft.com/how-we-do-it/ downloads*). This is how to choose what you need:
   a. In order to get a specific version, click "Customize your download."
   b. In the Product Version drop-down menu, select Version 7.1.5 or a later version. This book was written using version 7.1.5, and there are some small differences in the product if you use a later version.
   c. In the OS (Operating System) section, select your operating system. There are installers for Windows, Mac, and Linux. If you want to install on a different operating system, or if you do not want to use an installer, follow the Bonitasoft documentation on installing the OS-independent archive, and then go to "Starting Bonita BPM Studio" on page 11.
   d. In the Development section find the box labeled "Bonita BPM for *myOS*," where *myOS* is your operating system (Windows, Mac, or Linux).
   e. Click one of the buttons to download either the 32-bit or 64-bit version. If you are not sure which you need, download the 64-bit version because most recent systems are 64-bit. There is no 32-bit version for Mac.
   f. A popup asks whether you want to save the file. The filename starts with *BonitaBPMCommunity*. Click "Save file" and the file is stored in your default download location. This completes the download.
2. When you are ready to install the software, double-click the downloaded file to start the installer.
3. Choose your installation wizard language (in this chapter, we will use English), and click OK. This starts the setup wizard in your selected language.
4. Select the folder where you want to install the software, and then click Next. This concludes the setup steps.
5. To start the installation, click Next again. The installer installs the software in the location that you specified. Then it sets up your workspace, which is where your process and application files will be stored.
6. When the installer has finished, it gives you the option of launching the software. Check the box to launch it, and click Finish.
7. After a few minutes, the Bonita BPM Studio opens, and displays Figure 2-2.

Starting Bonita BPM Studio

After you have installed Bonita BPM Studio, you start it by going to the installation folder and double-clicking the launcher for your operating system. Depending on your operating system and the method you used to install the Studio, you will have one or more of the following launchers:

Operating system	Launcher
Linux	*BonitaBPMCommunity.sh* or *BonitaBPMCommunity64.sh*
Windows	*BonitaBPMCommunity.exe* or *BonitaBPMCommunity64.exe*
Mac	*BonitaBPMCommunity64.app*

If you install using the installation wizard on a 64-bit Linux or Windows system, you have a launcher called *BonitaBPMCommunity.sh* or *BonitaBPMCommunity.exe*: this is not an error, and the launcher works correctly on your 64-bit system.

The Bonita BPM Studio opens, and displays the Welcome page shown in Figure 2-2.

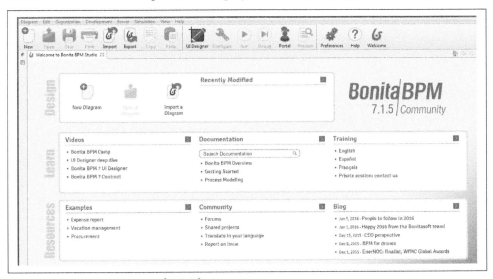

Figure 2-2. Bonita BPM Studio Welcome page

When you start the Studio for the first time, it creates database tables and initializes them, which takes a few minutes. The Recently Modified list will be empty if you have not used the Studio before.

If you installed Bonita BPM Studio using an installer, the Studio starts in the language you selected for the installation. If you did not use an installer, it starts in the default language of your operating system, or in English if that language is not supported. To change the Studio language to English, go to the top menu bar, click the Preferences icon and find the Language settings. There are two language configuration options; set them both to English. Of course, you can use the Studio in any of the available languages, but we recommend you use the English version while you are reading this book.

The following sections are quick visits to the key components of the Studio, to introduce the navigation terminology that is used throughout the rest of the book.

Diagram Editor

The Diagram Editor is the main Bonita BPM Studio view, and is used to update a process diagram. Click New Diagram, and you will see the view in Figure 2-3.

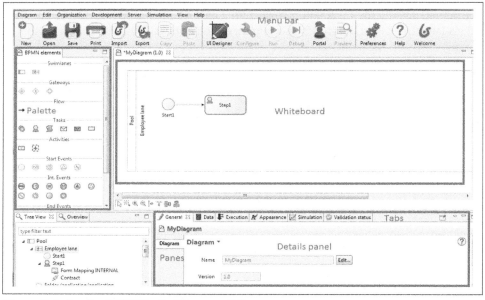

Figure 2-3. Bonita BPM Studio Diagram Editor

In this screen:

- The two-tier menu bar provides access to the actions possible with the Studio. The row of icons gives you quick access to the most frequently used actions.
- The palette contains icons for the BPMN elements that you use to model a process.
- The whiteboard is the drawing space where you assemble the icons from the palette to create a process diagram.
- The details panel is the space for configuring the process and the elements it contains. It is context-sensitive so the display changes based on the item selected in

the whiteboard. To navigate in the details panel, go first to a tab (along the top of the panel), then to a pane (down the left side of the tab).

UI Designer

The UI Designer is the Bonita BPM Studio component for creating and updating applications pages and forms. Click the UI Designer icon in the Studio toolbar, and you will see the UI Designer home page open in your browser (Figure 2-4):

Figure 2-4. UI Designer home page

In the "New page" box, enter the name of a page and press Return. This opens the Page Editor, which looks like Figure 2-5:

Figure 2-5. Bonita BPM Studio UI Designer Page Editor

In the Page Editor:

- The widget panel contains icons for the widgets that you use to construct a page.

- The whiteboard is the drawing space where you arrange widgets in a page.
- The variables panel is the space for creating the variables that determine the data displayed in the widgets and that control how the page behaves.
- The properties panel is the space for configuring each widget. It is context-sensitive so the display changes based on the item selected in the whiteboard.

Summary

You have seen the high-level needs statement of the example application that you will develop. You have installed the Bonita BPM software and are ready to get started on creating your vacation management application. In the next chapter, you will create a prototype of the application main page. You will also create the first version of the diagram for the process.

CHAPTER 3

Getting Started

In this chapter, you will create a prototype of the vacation statement, which is the application main page. You will also create the first version of the diagram for the process that is at the heart of the vacation management application.

Create the Application Prototype

In this section, you will create a prototype of the main page of the vacation management application. This is a critical step in validating the design with Helen, so it is good to do this right at the start of development. You can create a prototype page that uses dummy data but behaves like the final page.

Review "Example Application: Vacation Management" on page 7 in the previous chapter before you begin.

You need a title for the page, so first you can address Helen's requirement to give the application a cool name...

> Hi Helen, this is Fred from the IT development group. I've been looking at your requirements for the Vacation Management Application. I agree it's important to give it a cool name so everyone wants to use it. Something that says holidays, a sunny beach, blue ocean...Tahiti. Let's call it Tahiti!

A page is constructed from widgets, each widget corresponding to an item displayed on the screen. A widget has properties that determine its behavior. You can group widgets into a container and set some properties on the container. You can drag and drop widgets and containers to arrange them on the page.

The Tahiti application page has three sets of information:

- An introduction, which identifies the page and the current user.

- *My vacation*, showing the current user the details of their vacation requests and availability
- *Team vacation*, which is only displayed to managers, showing the current user the details of their team's vacation availability and a list of requests to review.

The following sections explain how to create the page with these sets of information, and how to create the variables and dummy data to test the page structure.

Create the Page and Add the Introduction

To create the prototype page, follow these steps:

1. In the Bonita BPM Studio Welcome page, click the UI Designer icon. This opens the UI Designer in your browser (Figure 3-1).

Figure 3-1. UI Designer home page

2. In the "New page" box, enter the name of the page you want to create, **TahitiVacationManagement**, and press Return. This opens the Page Editor with an empty whiteboard.
3. Drag a Container widget from the Widgets panel on the left side onto the whiteboard in the center of the screen. This will contain the page introduction, which is the name of the current user, the application title and logo, and some introductory text.
4. Drag a Text widget into the container. In the properties panel on the right of the whiteboard, change value of the Width property to 2 and change the Text property to **IMAGE**. This is a placeholder for a logo that you will add later.
5. Drag a Title widget into the container to the right of the IMAGE placeholder. Set the Width to 7. Set the Title level to Level 1. Set the Text to **Tahiti Vacation Management**.
6. Drag a Text widget into the container to the right of the title. Set the Text property to **username**.
7. Drag a Text widget into the container, below the title. This will create a new row. Set the Text property to a welcome message, something like this: *Welcome to the Tahiti Vacation Management Tool. Here you can see how many days of vacation*

you have available, see the status of your vacation requests, and submit a new vaca-tion request.

8. Drag another Text widget below the one that you just added. Set the Text prop-erty to a welcome message for managers, something like this: *If you are a man-ager, you can see the vacation status for your team and review pending requests.* Managers will see both welcome messages.

9. Click Save, and then click Preview. You will see something like Figure 3-2:

Figure 3-2. Preview of the Tahiti page prototype introduction

Add My Vacation Information

To add the information about the current user's vacation, first you will need to create variables. Variables are used to define the initial values of widgets. Variables are also used to store information such as the vacation request selected by the user, or to implement some logic in order to hide or display widgets.

We use JSON variables in the prototype to match the data format that will be used later when we will switch to API calls to set variable initial values from real data. You can learn more about JSON on json.org.

1. Create a JSON variable for the number of days of vacation available to the user. Follow these steps:

   a. In the Variables tab below the whiteboard, click "Create a new variable."

   b. Set the Name to **myVacationAvailable**.

   c. Set the Type to **JSON**.

   d. In the Value field, remove the braces that are added by default and enter the following:

   ```
   [{"daysAvailableCounter": 8}]
   ```

2. Create a JSON variable called **myVacation** with the following content:

   ```
   [{
     "requesterId": "3",
     "startDate": "2015-08-21T00:00:00.000Z",
     "numberOfDays": 2,
   ```

```
  "returnDate": "2015-08-22T00:00:00.000Z",
  "status": "pending"
}, {
  "requesterId": "3",
  "startDate": "2015-09-01T00:00:00.000Z",
  "numberOfDays": 4,
  "returnDate": "2015-09-07T00:00:00.000Z",
  "status": "approved"
}, {
  "requesterId": "3",
  "startDate": "2015-12-21T00:00:00.000Z",
  "numberOfDays": 4,
  "returnDate": "2015-12-28T00:00:00.000Z",
  "status": "pending"
}, {
  "requesterId": "3",
  "startDate": "2016-03-01T00:00:00.000Z",
  "numberOfDays": 4,
  "returnDate": "2016-03-04T00:00:00.000Z",
  "status": "approved"
}, {
  "requesterId": "3",
  "startDate": "2016-07-13T00:00:00.000Z",
  "numberOfDays": 1,
  "returnDate": "2016-07-22T00:00:00.000Z",
  "status": "refused"
}]
```

This is an array of five vacation requests that you can use an as example in previews of the application page.

3. Add a JSON variable called selectedRow with an empty value (do not enter a value; just leave the proposed Value field as it is, with empty braces, {}). This variable will be used to store information about the selected vacation request. It is also used to initialize the copySelectedRow variable, which you will create next.

4. When a user edits a vacation request we need to be sure that the original request information is left unchanged in the table. To do this, we need to have a copy of the selected row information. We create this copy by adding a JavaScript expression variable called copySelectedRow with the following value:

```
if($data.selectedRow.original !== null) {
    $data.selectedRow.copy =
  angular.copy($data.selectedRow.original);
    $data.selectedRow.original = null;
}
```

Now you can use the variables you have created in some page widgets:

1. Add a Container widget below the introduction container, to hold the information about the current user's vacation.
2. In the container, add a Title widget with Title level set to Level 2 and Text set to **My vacation**.
3. Below the title (but still inside the container), add an Input widget. Check the radio button to make this field read-only. Set the Label to **Vacation days available**. Set the Label position to **left**. Set the Value to point to `myVacationAvaila ble[0].daysAvailableCounter`. `myVacationAvailable` is an array that contains a single object; this object has one attribute named `daysAvailableCounter` that stores the number of vacation days available for the current user. When you start typing, the matching variable names are displayed and you can select `myVacatio nAvailableNumber` from the list. Note that completion is not available for the attributes of variables.
4. In the same row as the Input widget, add a Link widget. Set the Style property to **primary**, which makes the link look like a button. Set the Width property to 4. Set the Text property to **Create new vacation request**. You can ignore the other properties, because in this prototype the link is not clickable. In the real application, the user will click this button to go to the form to create a new vacation request.
5. Add a Table widget with the following properties:

Property	Setting
Headers	*Start date, Number of days, Return date, Status*
Content	Bind (click *fx* button) to the variable `myVacation`
Column keys	*startDate	date, numberOfDays, returnDate	date, status*
Selected row	Bind to the variable *selectedRow.original*

6. Below the table, add two Date picker widgets, labeled **Start date** and **Return date**. Set the width for each to 4 so they are in the same row. Set the Value properties to **selectedRow.copy.startDate** and **selectedRow.copy.returnDate**, respectively. These widgets should be hidden if no row is selected, so set the Hidden property for each one. To do this, go to the property, click *fx*, and in the field that appears, enter this expression: **!selectedRow.copy**. This is called binding the property to the value of the expression.
7. Beside the Return date widget add an Input widget. Set the Label to **Number of days**. Set the Value to **selectedRow.copy.numberOfDays** and the Type to **number**. Bind the Hidden property to `!selectedRow.copy`.
8. On a new row add two Button widgets, labeled **Cancel selected vacation** and **Modify selected vacation**. Set the width for each to 6 so they are in the same row. Set the alignment of the Cancel button to **right**. These buttons are hidden unless

a relevant vacation request is selected in the table, so you need to set conditions that control when to display the buttons, as follows:

- For the "Modify selected vacation" button, bind the Hidden property to `selec tedRow.copy.status!=="pending"`. This means that if the status of the selected request is not pending, or if no request is selected, the button is hidden.
- For the "Cancel selected vacation" button, bind the Hidden property to:

    ```
    !(selectedRow.copy && selectedRow.copy.status=="refused")
    ```

    This means that the button is hidden if no request is selected, or if the selected request was refused.

9. If you are using Bonita BPM 7.0.* or 7.1.*, you need to add a workaround to initialize the `copySelectedRow` variable. Add an Input widget and set the Value to **copySelectedRow**. Hide the widget by setting the CSS classes property to **visibility: hidden**.
10. Click Save, and then click Preview. The "Cancel selected vacation" and "Modify selected vacation" buttons are only displayed when a relevant vacation request is selected in the table. For example, if you select the first pending request, you will see something like Figure 3-3.

In the Preview, if you select an approved request, the "Cancel selected vacation" button is displayed, but the "Modify selected vacation" button is not because you cannot modify an approved request. If you select a request that was refused, no buttons are displayed.

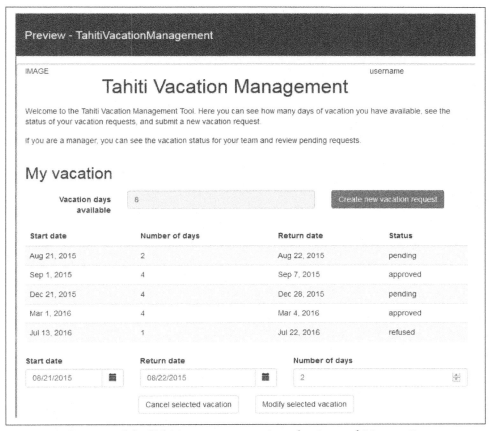

Figure 3-3. Preview of the Tahiti page prototype introduction and My vacation

Add Team Vacation Information

Before you can add the vacation information about the current user's team members you need to create two new variables:

- Create a JSON variable called `managerTeamInfo` with the following content:

```
{
  "isManager": true,
  "employeesVacationRequests": [{
    "firstName": "April",
    "lastName": "Sanchez",
    "startDate": "2015-12-09T00:00:00.000Z",
    "returnDate": "2015-12-11T00:00:00.000Z",
    "numberOfDays": 2,
    "status": "approved",
    "taskId": "123"
```

```
  }, {
    "firstName": "April",
    "lastName": "Sanchez",
    "startDate": "2015-09-01T00:00:00.000Z",
    "returnDate": "2015-09-07T00:00:00.000Z",
    "numberOfDays": 4,
    "status": "pending",
    "taskId": "456"
  }, {
    "firstName": "Walter",
    "lastName": "Bates",
    "startDate": "2015-11-09T00:00:00.000Z",
    "returnDate": "2015-11-12T00:00:00.000Z",
    "numberOfDays": 2,
    "status": "pending",
    "taskId": "789"
  }],
  "employeesVacationAvailable": [{
    "firstName": "Walter",
    "lastName": "Bates",
    "daysAvailableCounter": 6
  }, {
    "firstName": "April",
    "lastName": "Sanchez",
    "daysAvailableCounter": 18
  }]
}
```

This is a complex JSON object that stores all the information about team vacation for a manager:

— isManager indicates whether the current user is a manager based on organization information. This variable attribute will be used in conjunction with the Hidden property to determine whether to show or hide the information that is only relevant for managers. In the real application page, the value will be set by referencing information about the current user, but in the prototype, you will set the value to true or false as a shortcut.

— employeesVacationRequests provides the list of vacation requests for employees managed by the current user.

— employeesVacationAvailable provides the list of vacation available for the employees managed by the current user.

• Create a JSON variable called teamSelectedRow with no content (just empty {} braces).

Now you can use these variables you have created in some page widgets.

First, use the managerTeamInfo.isManager variable to set a condition on the manager welcome message that you have already created, by configuring the Hidden property.

When `managerTeamInfo.isManager` is false, Hidden evaluates to true and the manager welcome message is not displayed. Follow these steps:

1. Select the manager welcome message widget and go to the Properties panel on the right of the whiteboard.
2. In the Hidden property, click the bind icon at the right of the field, then enter this value:

    ```
    managerTeamInfo.isManager==false
    ```

3. Check that the condition on the manager welcome message is defined correctly:
    a. Edit the `managerTeamInfo` variable by clicking the Edit icon in the Variables tab and setting the `isManager` attribute value to **false**.
    b. Save the page and preview it. The manager welcome message (*You can also see...*) should not be displayed.
    c. Edit the `managerTeamInfo` variable again and set the `isManager` attribute value back to true.

Now add new widgets to display the team vacation requests information:

1. At the bottom of the page add a Container widget. In the container properties, bind the Hidden property to the same value that you used for the manager welcome message:

    ```
    managerTeamInfo.isManager==false
    ```

    This means that the container will be displayed to users who are managers, but will be hidden otherwise.
2. Add a Title widget with Title level set to Level 2 and Text set to **Team vacation**.
3. Add a Tabs container inside the container. By default, two tabs are created. Click each tab in turn and change the Title property, so that the tabs are labeled **Vacation available** and **Vacation requests**.
4. Configure the Vacation available tab by adding a Table widget with the following properties:

Property	Setting
Headers	*First name, Last name, Days available*
Content	*Bind to the variable managerTeamInfo.employeesVacationAvailable*
Column keys	*firstName, lastName, daysAvailableCounter*

Save and preview the page. The team vacation available information will look something like Figure 3-4.

Figure 3-4. Preview of the Tahiti page prototype team vacation availability

5. Configure the Vacation requests tab by adding the following:

- A Table widget with the following properties:

Property	Setting
Headers	*First name, Last name, Start date, Number of days, Return date, Status*
Content	Bind to the variable *managerTeamInfo.employeesVacationRequests*
Column keys	*firstName, lastName, startDate	date, numberOfDays, returnDate	date, status*
Selected row	Bind to the variable *teamSelectedRow*

- A Link widget with the following properties:

Property	Setting
Hidden	Bind to *teamSelectedRow.status!=="pending"*
Text	*Review selected vacation request*
Alignment	*center*
Style	*primary*

You can ignore the other properties because in the prototype page the button is not clickable.

6. Click Save, then click Preview. In the preview, you can switch to a tab by clicking the tab title. The team vacation requests information will look something like Figure 3-5:

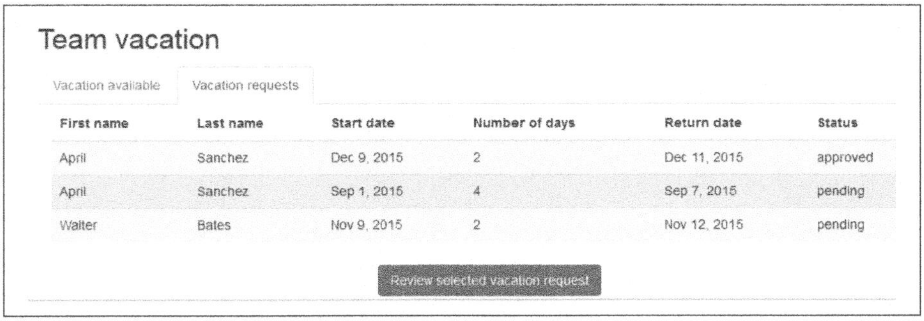

Figure 3-5. Preview of the Tahiti page prototype team pending vacation requests

7. Go to the Variables tab and temporarily change the value of the `managerTea mInfo.isManager` variable to false. Preview the page again and verify that the manager welcome message and the team vacation container are hidden.

When you have configured all the information in the page, the whiteboard view of the page in the Page Editor will look something like Figure 3-6.

You have now completed the prototype page for the Tahiti application. You can validate the design with Helen, then start work on the process diagrams.

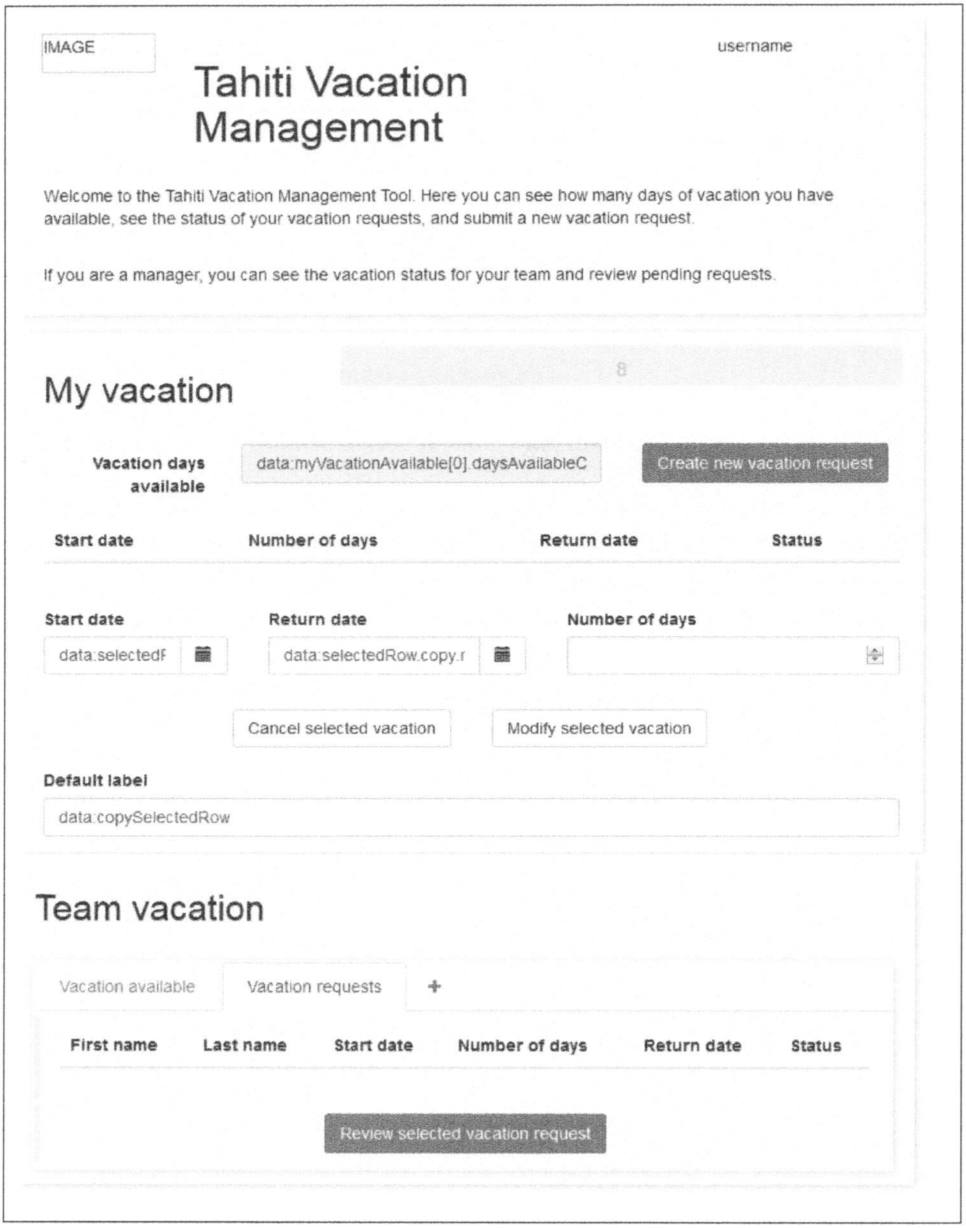

Figure 3-6. Tahiti page prototype in the Page Editor whiteboard

Create Your First Process Diagram

In this section, you will create your first process diagram. This is just the first iteration, and the diagram will be updated and refined in subsequent chapters as you learn what the components mean. For now, though, your goals are to get used to using the Studio, and to get a quick visual representation of the process that is at the heart of the application, without worrying about the details.

When you update a process definition or other information in the Studio, save your work from time to time by clicking the Save icon in the top bar or by typing Ctrl-S.

Follow these instructions to create a BPMN diagram that is equivalent to Figure 2-1:

1. In the Bonita BPM Studio Welcome page, click the New Diagram icon. This creates the beginning of a new process diagram and opens it for edit (see Figure 3-7).

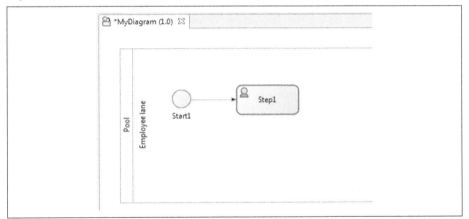

Figure 3-7. New diagram in Bonita BPM Studio

2. Give your diagram a name (instead of the default, *MyDiagram*):

   a. Click on the whiteboard outside the diagram, then go to the Details panel and click the Edit button next to the Name field. A popup opens, as shown in Figure 3-8.

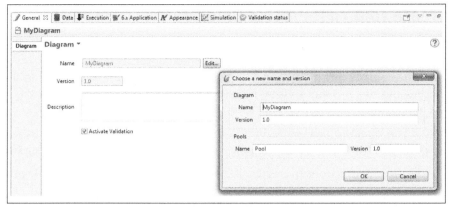

Figure 3-8. Renaming a diagram in Bonita BPM Studio

b. In the popup, enter the name for the diagram, **Tahiti-NewVacationRequest**, and a new name for the Pool, **New Vacation Request**. You will find out more later about pools and lanes and why they are useful. For now, just change the name from the default, Pool, so you can identify it later. Now your diagram looks like Figure 3-9:

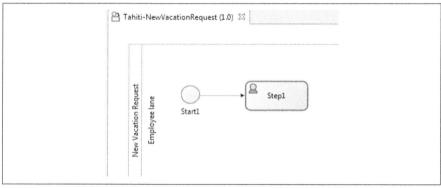

Figure 3-9. Renamed diagram in Bonita BPM Studio

3. Create the task where an employee submits a vacation request. The diagram already contains a human task, called Step1, so you can just rename it:

a. Click Step1 to select it, and go to the Details panel.
b. In the Name field, enter the new name for the step, **Submit vacation request**. The new name appears on the step in the whiteboard.

This task is a placeholder for a form that you will add later.

4. Add the task where the employee's manager reviews the request:

a. Go to the BPMN elements palette on the left of the whiteboard, click the icon for a human task, and drag it to the whiteboard. When you drop the icon, it creates a new task and selects it.

b. Go to the Details panel and enter the name for the step, **Review request.**

5. Connect the request step to the review step:

a. Click the request step to select it. You will see some icons at the edge of the selected area. This is called the context palette (Figure 3-10).

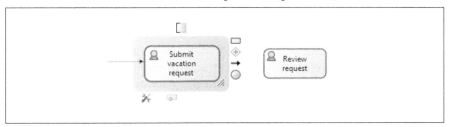

Figure 3-10. The selected step is highlighted

b. Click the link icon (the arrow on the right of the task) and drag it to the review task. This creates a link between the two tasks.

6. There is one more task in the process, but it applies only if the manager refuses a request, so first you need a branch point to represent this condition. Branch points are known as gateways, and here you need an exclusive (XOR) gateway. You will come back to gateways in more detail in Chapter 8. To add the gateway:

a. Go to the BPMN elements palette and find the icon for an XOR gateway.

b. Drag the icon to the whiteboard and drop it after the review step.

c. Connect the review step to the gateway by selecting the step and dragging the link arrow to the gateway.

7. Change the name of the gateway by selecting the gateway in the whiteboard and entering the name in the Details panel. Call the gateway **Request approved?.**

8. Add a task for informing HR when a request is refused. This is an automatic task that sends an email message. It is done by the system, not a person. The procedure for adding the service task is the same as for the review task (step 4), but this time you need to select the service task icon. Name this task **Notify HR request refused.**

9. Connect the gateway to the HR task. Then add a label, *no*, to the link, by selecting the link and entering the label in the Name field in the Details panel. Now your diagram looks something like Figure 3-11:

Figure 3-11. The diagram contains all the steps

10. To finish the diagram, all you need to add are the ends. There are two ways this process ends: after the manager approves the request, and after the manager's refusal is logged with HR.

   a. First, add the end after approval. To do this, find the terminate end event icon in the BPMN elements palette, drag it to the whiteboard, and drop it below the gateway. Then add a link from the gateway to the end point, and label it *yes*.

   b. Now add the end after the HR notification task. To do this, drag the terminate end event icon from the palette to the whiteboard and drop it beside the task, and add a link from the task to the end point.

Now the first version of the diagram is finished, and looks like Figure 3-12:

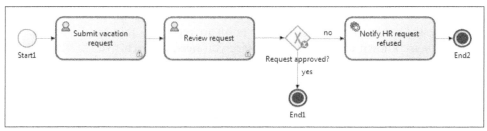

Figure 3-12. The first iteration of the diagram is complete

Notice the dot on the gateway. This indicates that there is an error in the gateway configuration, because the condition test for which branch to take is not yet defined. You will complete this in Chapter 8. The triangles are warnings; they indicate that some required information is not specified, so it is normal to see warnings at this stage when the diagram is incomplete. You can ignore them for now, but remember to check that there are no warnings in your final process diagram.

Run the Process

At any time while you are developing a process diagram, you can run the process by clicking the Run icon on the top bar. You can run the process now to check for errors, even though at this early stage it does not display any useful forms or produce any results. It is a good idea to run the process after each change to make sure that no errors have been introduced.

Summary

You have created a prototype of the vacation statement, which is the application main page. You have also created the first version of the diagram for the process that is at the heart of the vacation management application. Even at this early stage, the diagram is the key reference for everyone involved in the application development, to make sure that the process specification is correct and clear.

The next chapter looks at how this process is started and stopped, and how it fits into the Tahiti application as a whole.

CHAPTER 4

Managing Starts and Stops

In the previous chapter, you created the first version of the process diagram, matching the basic flow that was described in the requirements.

This chapter considers the overall structure of the Tahiti application, and how the processes within the application start and stop. Helen's description of the vacation management application that she wants is broken down into a user experience description of the visible elements application, including the usage pattern of each element (what, who, how). This is then used to define the components of the application, how they are related, and how they are started and stopped. At the end of the chapter, you will update the diagram to include more process components.

User Experience Description

This section contains the application description broken down into a set of descriptions of the visible parts of the application, with details of the usage pattern of each one, and an extract of the requirement from Helen.

Application Page with Vacation Statement

What: A summary of days available, booked, and taken, then a table showing requests. Team information for managers. Button to modify or cancel pending vacation requests. Button to cancel an approved vacation request. Button to open a form to create a new request. This is what Helen asked for:

> ...display the number of days I have available to book, and the number of days booked but not yet taken. This is a kind of "vacation statement," like a bank statement but for my vacation days! From this page, I want to click a button and fill in a form to request vacation.

Who: All users.

How: Log in to the application, and this is what you see.

Vacation Request Form

What: A form for requesting vacation. Helen said she wants to fill in a form to request vacation.

Who: All users.

How: Click button on vacation statement to access this form. Complete the form and click Submit button to send request to manager for review.

Vacation Modification Option

What: A form to modify a previously submitted vacation request, for vacation that has not been approved. Has the details of the original request pre-filled.

Who: All users

How: Select vacation request in vacation statement and click a button to see a modification form, which is added to the application page.

Vacation Cancellation Option

What: A button in the vacation statement, used to cancel or request cancellation of previously booked vacation.

Who: All users.

How: Select vacation request in vacation statement and click a button. If the request is pending, it is just cancelled. If it is already approved, the cancellation request is sent to the manager for approval.

Notification for Manager of Pending Request

What: An automatic notification sent by email to the manager of someone who submits a vacation request, requesting review and approval. Helen was not specific about how the manager should be informed that there is a request to review:

> The request is sent to my manager, who reviews it and approves or refuses it.

Who: All managers.

How: Email is sent automatically.

Vacation Request Review Form

What: The form that a manager uses to review a vacation request and decide whether to approve or refuse it. Similar forms are used for new requests and for cancellation. This is what Helen asked for:

> As a manager, when I get a request to review, I need to be able to check at a glance that the requester is using up vacation sensibly so that there isn't a big backlog at the end of the year.

Who: All managers.

How: In the vacation statement for a manager, select a pending request and click the button to open the review form.

Team Vacation Statement for Manager

What: A list of all the members of a team and the number of vacation days that they have available. This is what Helen asked for:

> I need some kind of a vacation statement for the whole team, just available to the manager.

Who: All managers.

How: If you are a manager, your vacation statement includes your team vacation information as well as your own.

Calendar Interaction

What: In the team calendar, everyone can see when a team member has booked vacation. This was Helen's description of what she needs:

> I need approved vacation to be added automatically to the team calendar, so that the whole team can see at a glance who is in work on any date. It would be useful if requested vacation could be in the calendar too, but marked as provisional. That way when I review a request, I can check that there are not too many people absent at the same time.

Who: All users.

How: Calendar is updated automatically when a request is submitted, approved, refused, modified, or cancelled.

HR Tracking of Refusals

What: Some way of tracking requests that are refused. This is what Helen needs for the HR team:

> I need a way to check refusals in case an employee complains that a refusal was unfair... We need some kind of tracking of refused requests with the reason for the refusal.

Who: HR.

How: When a manager refuses a vacation request, email is sent to HR. The email notification of refusal has a defined format of subject. Configure your email system to detect this and automatically file the messages.

Component Definitions

Now that we have described the elements of the Tahiti application from the users' point of view, we need to create a high-level specification for each component, including how they are related. Most of the elements that users see are web pages and forms, but there are processes and other components that connect them together logically or in code, and other components that generate the information that is displayed. This is the set of components that you will create using this book, for the first implementation of the Tahiti application.

Home Page

The key page in the application is the vacation statement. You have already created a prototype for this. "Update the Vacation Statement" on page 86 explains how to convert this prototype into the page that will be the Tahiti application home page.

There are also the forms used in the processes. Chapter 7 explains how to create forms for the processes.

Login

If you were putting Tahiti into production, you would probably access it through your corporate intranet using single sign-on, but for this version, users will log in through Bonita BPM Portal, then access the application by URL.

Vacation statement

This is the landing page that a user sees after login. You created a prototype in "Create the Application Prototype" on page 15. It shows vacation requests that are pending and approved. It has buttons to start a new request, and to request modification or cancellation of a pending or approved request.

For a manager, the vacation statement is extended to include information about vacation available and pending requests for team members.

Vacation Request Process

In this chapter, you will consider only the default paths of a new vacation request.

The request process contains these elements:

- A human task with a form for creating the new vacation request
- A human task with a form for the manager review of the request
- An email notification of approval sent to the requester
- An email notification of refusal sent to the requester
- An email notification of refusal sent to HR

In the next section, you will update the diagram to show these elements, first updating the tasks and then adding the tasks where email notifications are sent.

In the final Tahiti application, there will also be processes to handle modification and cancellation of a vacation request, and a process to initialize the data used. You will add these in later chapters, after you have created the basic process for submitting and reviewing a request.

Updating the Process Diagram

You need to update the diagram to modify the task at the start of the process, and to add the notification tasks.

Updating the Human Tasks

The diagram already shows the two tasks, *Submit vacation request* for a user creating a new vacation request, and *Review request* for the manager reviewing the request.

When a user submits a new vacation request, this creates a process instance. This instance continues to exist until the manager approves or refuses the vacation request and the process reaches one of the ends you defined in the diagram. Submitting a new vacation request is the *process instantiation* action, so it is defined at the pool level, not in a human task. The process instance does not exist until the vacation request is submitted. Update the diagram as follows:

1. Remove the human task called *Submit vacation request* by selecting it and choosing Delete from the right-mouse-button menu (or pressing the Delete key).
2. Connect the Start icon to the *Review request* task.
3. There is no task icon for the process instantiation action, so we recommend you add a text annotation to indicate that the form is needed. To add a text annotation, drag the icon from the palette and drop it on the whiteboard before the Start icon. You can put whatever text you want in a text annotation. In this case, add a note that the vacation request form is used for process instantiation.

The *Review request* task does not need to be changed, but you can add a text annotation here also, indicating that a form is needed. In this case, add a link from the text annotation to the human task to show they are connected. To do this, select the annotation and drag the arrow to the task.

Your diagram should now look like Figure 4-1:

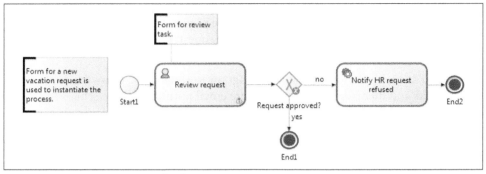

Figure 4-1. Text annotations for forms

Adding Notification Tasks

A notification task is a *service task*. You need to add service tasks after the *Request approved?* gateway:

- To inform the user that the request is approved, add a task called *Notify employee request approved* to the *yes* branch.
- To inform the user that the request is refused, add a task called *Notify employee request refused* to the *no* branch.

You have already created the *Notify HR request refused* task on the *no* branch.

Add each missing service task as follows:

1. Drag the service task icon from the palette and drop it on the relevant link out of the gateway. This inserts the task in the middle of the link.
2. Optionally, rearrange the diagram to make the layout less crowded.
3. Change the task name to describe the notification.
4. Add a text annotation for the task with a note that the task will send an email message automatically. To do this, click the task to display the context palette, and then drag and drop the Text annotation widget. This creates a text annotation that is linked to the task. Enter the text you want in the annotation. You can enlarge the annotation box so that all the text is visible in the diagram.

Your diagram should now look like Figure 4-2:

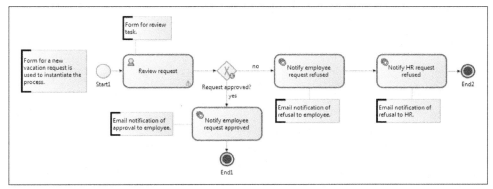

Figure 4-2. Text annotations for email notifications

Chapter 12 explains how to configure a service task to send an email message.

Summary

In this chapter, you have added more items to the diagram, and used text annotations to mark the places where you need to add a form or configure a service task to send an email message.

The next chapter explains how to define who carries out the activities in the process.

CHAPTER 5

Assigning Tasks

The previous chapter described all the components of the Tahiti application and how each one starts and stops.

This chapter shows you how to specify who is permitted to start a process instance and which users can perform each task in a process. You will update the process diagram to specify who is permitted to start an instance of the process and who is permitted to carry out each human task. There are several layers of decisions:

- In the process diagram, you specify placeholders (actors) and some logical definitions (actor filter specification).
- When you configure a process for deployment you map the placeholders to sets of users (actor mapping).
- When the process runs, the live information is used (actor filter evaluation).

The BPMN standard defines a *Performer*, which specifies the resource that can perform an activity. For a human task, the resource is a person. The performer can be specified as an individual, a group, an organizational role or position, or any combination of these criteria.

The standard does not define a way to show performers in the diagram. However, it does define the concept of a *lane*. The container for a process in a diagram is a *pool*. You can divide a pool into several lanes (think swimlanes in a swimming pool). A lane can be used to organize a diagram into whatever categories you find useful, and the standard contains an example of lanes that match groups within an organization.

This chapter deals with who does what in a process, but does not consider Tahiti components that are not part of a process, like the vacation statement page. Access to these pages is controlled by login credentials, and is explained in Chapter 10.

Actors

In Bonita BPM, you use a combination of the organization definition and actors to specify who performs human tasks in a process. The organization definition contains all the people in your organization, along with the groups they belong to and the roles they have. The simplest way to structure this is to match it to your corporate hierarchy, though this is not mandatory. Your organization definition also needs to include any users outside your company who participate in processes, such as suppliers. Bonita BPM Studio contains an example organization structure, which you can use for testing while you develop a process. To see the example and how it is defined, go to the Organization menu and choose Manage. You will find Helen and her team, and the rest of the ACME employees.

You assign an actor to a lane as a placeholder for the people who can perform the human tasks in the lane. The advantage of this is that it gives a visual representation of the tasks carried out by the same actor. You are recommended to choose lane names and actor names that are clearly connected.

You can also specify an actor for a human task. This overrides the definition for the lane.

To convert the actor-placeholders into names of real people, you use actor mapping. You can map an actor to a part of the organization by specifying a group, a role, or group and role. You can also map an actor to a specific person, though this is not recommended. The mapping means that you can update your organization whenever you have a change in staffing, when an employee joins the company, switches roles internally, or leaves the company, but you do not need to update the process definitions. When a process runs, it always uses the current organization information to evaluate the actor mapping.

Filtering

After you have specified the actor for a human task, either explicitly or in the lane, you can override this by specifying an actor filter. An actor filter can either refine the actor definition or replace it completely.

An actor filter is specified in the process diagram, but is evaluated at runtime. This means that the filter can use information about the specific process instance. For example, if you assign the manager actor to the *Review request* task, this is not a sufficiently precise definition: the task needs to be performed by the manager of the employee who submitted the vacation request.

An actor filter can also use external system information.

Example

Suppose that the new Tahiti application is going to be tested by the employees in the HR department before it is put into production. Helen Kelly is the manager of the HR group. She belongs to the HR group and has the manager role. April Sanchez is a member of the HR group, and reports to Helen.

This is the logic sequence for determining who carries out activities when someone submits a vacation request:

Actor

> In the process diagram, the *Employee* lane is mapped to the Employee actor.

Actor filter definition

> The Employee actor is assigned to the *Review request* task (because this is the default actor). An actor filter is defined for the task, specifying that *Review request* task must be carried out by the manager of the person who submitted the request.

Actor mapping

> When the process is configured and ready for testing to start, the Employee actor is mapped to the HR group. This means that anyone in the HR group can start a process instance by submitting a vacation request.

Actor filter evaluation

> After a process instance is started, the identity of the requester is known, so when the actor filter is evaluated, the manager is identified and the task is assigned to them. If April submits a vacation request, Helen is asked to review it.

Updating the Process Diagram

In this section, you will update the process diagram to add a lane for each type of user, and then specify the actors for each lane.

There is already a default lane for *Employees*, so you just need to add lanes for *Manager* and *HR*. To add the *Manager* lane:

1. Go to the palette and drag the swimlane icon onto the diagram. You can drop it anywhere on the background inside the pool. The new lane is added to the diagram.
2. Click inside the new lane to select it.
3. Go to the Details panel, General tab, Lane pane.
4. In the Name field, specify the name of the lane, ***Manager lane***.

Do the same to add the *HR* lane.

Example | 43

Now move the diagram elements into the relevant lane by dragging and dropping them. When you do this, the links between elements usually get tangled. It is easier to move all the elements first, then move the links to make them tidier. It is not essential to keep your diagram tidy, but it makes it much easier to maintain and to collaborate with other process developers.

The position of a service task is not connected to any actor definition. However, a service task is usually done on behalf of an actor, so it is useful to position it in the lane for that actor. In your diagram, position a service task that sends an email message in the lane of the person whose actions cause the message to be sent.

When you have finished, your diagram should look like Figure 5-1:

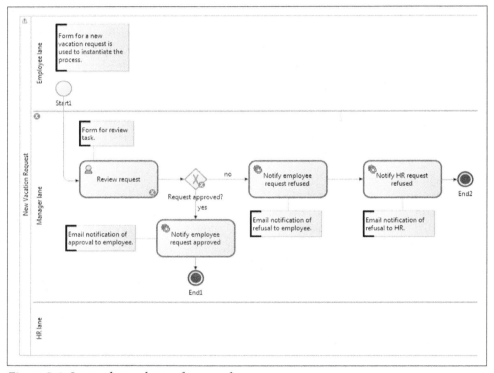

Figure 5-1. Lanes show who performs tasks

Notice that the *HR* lane is empty. This is because HR receives information from the process but does not take any actions. It is still useful to keep the empty lane as a visible reminder that HR is involved in the process.

During development, while the process definition is unfinished, it is completely normal to see error and warning indicators. Generally these indicate where the definition is not yet complete, so they are useful reminders. However, you should check them from time to time to make sure that you have not introduced any errors. To list all the errors and warnings, go to the Details panel, Validation status tab, and click Refresh.

Tips for Updating a Diagram

Tidy diagrams are easier to maintain. Here are some tips to help you keep your diagram tidy when you are updating it.

Space

When you add lanes to a diagram, it can quickly become bigger than the default size of the whiteboard, even if you are displaying Bonita BPM Studio at full screen. You can change the size of the whiteboard by dragging the bottom and left-side borders. You can also use the Maximize/Minimize icons at the top-right of the whiteboard to switch between the default view and a view that shows only the whiteboard.

There is also an option in the View menu to reduce the size of the icons in the toolbar to leave more space on your screen for the whiteboard.

Pool size

You can make a pool bigger or smaller by selecting it and clicking the plus or minus icons that appear around the perimeter.

Alignment

When you drag an element around the whiteboard, red horizontal and vertical guide-rules appear as elements get near to alignment, and disappear again when elements are not aligned. When you see the guide-rules, move the element slowly until it is aligned as you want.

Alternatively, you can switch the mouse pointer from "selection" mode to "vertical alignment" or "horizontal alignment." You need to click the appropriate icon at the bottom left of the whiteboard and select the elements to align. For selection you can either hold down the Ctrl key and click elements to select or you can use the selection box to select several elements. When you have finished aligning elements, remember to switch back to "selection" mode (the default) by clicking the default pointer icon.

Chronology

A process diagram does not show chronology. However, for simplicity, it is preferable to keep one direction for forward! With the exception of loops, avoid having links that go "back."

Assigning Actors and Filters

Now that you have created the lanes, the next step is to assign actors to the human tasks.

In the *Employee* lane, there are no visible human tasks, but an actor must be specified for the lane to define who can start an instance of the process. In this case, the actor that you need to assign, Employee, is already assigned to the lane by default, so no action is necessary.

To see the actor that is assigned to a lane:

1. Click the lane to select it.
2. Go to the Details panel, General tab, Actors pane.
3. The "Select an actor" line shows the actor that is currently assigned. You can change this using the drop-down menu. If there is no suitable actor defined, you can add an actor by clicking the Add button.

In the *Manager* lane, use an actor filter to assign the review task to the manager of the employee who submitted the request. To do this:

1. Click the *Manager* lane to select it.
2. Go to the Details panel, General tab, Actors pane.
3. In the "Select an actor" line, choose the Employee actor from the drop-down list.
4. Next to "Actor filter," click the Set button. A popup opens.
5. In the list on the right, click "Initiator manager" to select it.
6. Click Next.
7. Enter a name, *requesterManager*, for the actor filter.
8. Click Next.
9. Check the box for "Assign task automatically."
10. Click Finish.

The result of this is that when an employee submits a vacation request, which initiates the process, the employee's manager is identified by the process and is automatically assigned the review task.

In the *HR* lane there are no human tasks, so it is not necessary to assign an actor.

Summary

You have updated the diagram to specify who carries out the human tasks, adding visual information about the people impacted by the elements in the process.

The next chapter describes how to define the data model for your application.

CHAPTER 6

Using Data

The previous chapter showed you how to define who carries out tasks in a process. This chapter shows you how to define the data that is required for the Tahiti application. The BPMN standard does not specifically deal with data, but it is not surprising that you need data to make a process work. Data is the reason that applications and processes exist. Most processes require data as input and produce data as output. You need to define a data model that applies to all the components of the Tahiti application, not just to the processes.

The data model is defined as a set of Java objects. If you are not familiar with the concept of objects, do not worry about this. Just think of an object as a template, like a template for a document. From the template, you can create any number of documents, each one different but all following the same pattern.

Data Use Patterns

When defining the data model for a process or an application, you need to think about the lifetime of the data and where it is used. The answer to these questions determines where it needs to be stored.

Lifetime
> Does the data exist before a process instance starts? Does it exist before a user starts the application? Does it continue to exist after the process is complete or the application stops?

Use
> Is the data used only in one process or application, or in many? Does it have the same value in all cases of a process, or is it case-specific? Is it used by external information system (IS) components?

Information that is used in several processes or applications should be defined as business data. This is stored in a business data database and is available to all processes and applications running on your platform. This data can only be updated from within a process.

Information that is used by external IS components must be stored in an external system, and accessed by the application when needed. Typically, information is stored where it is "owned." For example, a travel planner application could access a database of available train or plane times.

The Tahiti application needs the following types of data:

- Business data, storing available vacation and requests. This is defined in the business data model. Business data is a Bonita BPM concept, not a BPMN concept. First you need to define the business data model, and then you define the parts of the model that are used in each process.
- Organization data, used to control access to the application, to route approval tasks to the requester's manager, and to display information for a team.

There is also data that is associated with an application page or form, but we will come back to that in a later chapter.

Defining the Business Data Model

The business data model (BDM) applies to all the processes and applications on your Bonita BPM system. For this reason, when you make changes you are asked to confirm whether to apply the updated model, in case it causes errors in other deployed processes. When you are developing your first application, you can safely ignore these warnings. Subsequently, you must make sure that any changes to the model are backward-compatible.

This section explains how to create the data model for the whole Tahiti application, including the processes for modifying and cancelling vacation requests, which you have not yet defined.

Data Model Design Choices

You do not need to understand why we made the choices we did in creating the data model for the Tahiti application. However, a short explanation might help when you come to extend the model for your future processes. Skip to the next section if you are not interested!

Objects and their lifecycles

We decided to use two objects, one for a vacation request (so a user will create many instances) and one to store the available vacation for each user (so there are as many instances as there are employees). In an integrated system of HR processes, the available vacation would probably be stored in some external database, so using a separate object makes it easier to migrate to this later.

Process information inside the vacation request object

A business object can only be updated by a process instance. When a user action on the Tahiti application page triggers an update, there needs to be a way to identify the relevant process instance. We decided to include the ID of the request process instance inside the request object, so that it is readily available in the Tahiti application page. The alternative is to use a search of all the current process instances to find the relevant instance.

Business Objects

For Tahiti, you need to define two objects:

- VacationRequest, which contains these attributes:
  — requesterBonitaBPMId (Long)
  — reviewerBonitaBPMId (Long)
  — startDate (Date)
  — returnDate (Date)
  — numberOfDays (Integer)
  — status (String)
  — comments (String)
  — calendarEventId (String)
  — newRequestProcessInstanceId (Long)
- VacationAvailable, which contains these attributes:
  — bonitaBPMId (Long)
  — daysAvailableCounter (Integer)

There is also an attribute called persistenceId that is added automatically to all objects. It is an identifier for an instance of an object. You do not need to specify it when defining an object, but you can use it in queries.

To define the business data model, follow these steps:

1. In Bonita BPM Studio, go to the Development menu, choose Business Data Model, then choose Manage. A popup opens.
2. Go to the List of Business Objects and click Add. A temporary object name, such as BusinessObject1, is added to the list.
3. Click the temporary name and replace it with **VacationRequest**.
4. Click VacationRequest to select it, ready to add a description and its attributes.

5. In the Description field, add a description. The description is optional but recommended, because it is useful for later maintenance of the model. Even self-explanatory object names can become less obvious over time!

6. In the Attributes tab, click Add to add an attribute. A temporary attribute name, such as `attribute1`, is added to the attribute list.

7. Click the temporary attribute, which is added automatically, and change its name to `requesterBonitaBPMId`. Set the Type to LONG.

8. Click Add and then add the remaining attributes.

9. When you have added all the attributes, specify which ones are mandatory by checking the relevant boxes in the Mandatory column: they are all mandatory except `reviewerBonitaBPMId`, `comments`, and `calendarEventId`. When you have finished, the dialog box will look like Figure 6-1:

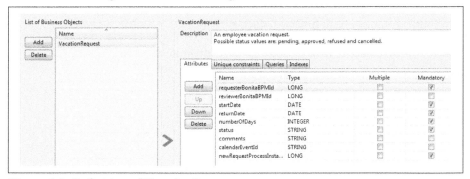

Figure 6-1. Definition of VacationRequest

10. Repeat the procedure to add the `VacationAvailable` object. Both its attributes are mandatory. The definition should look like Figure 6-2:

Figure 6-2. Definition of VacationAvailable

11. Add a uniqueness constraint on the `bonitaBPMId` attribute of the `VacationAvail able` object so that you are sure that only one counter exists for each user. This is an extra test to guarantee data consistency. To add the constraint:

   a. In the List of Business Objects, select `VacationAvailable`.

   b. Go to the Unique constraints tab and click Add.

c. Change the Name to `uniqueBonitaBPMId`.
   d. Click in the Attributes column, then click the (...) button that appears on the right. This opens a popup with the list of attributes in the `VacationAvailable` object.
   e. Check the box to select the `bonitaBPMId` attribute, and then click OK.

Optionally, you can change the data model package name, which is the name used to reference the model from scripts and code. This book uses the default name, `com.company.model`. You can change this to use your own company name.

You have now defined the objects that you need in your data model for the Tahiti application. The next section explains how to specify the queries used to retrieve instances of these objects.

Queries

To retrieve data stored in the business database you use queries. Queries are defined for each object declared in the business data model. A query might require parameters, which are used to filter the list of selected data objects.

A set of default queries is available for each object type in the model. There is a query for each attribute of the object type, which retrieves a list of objects where the attribute has a given value. There is also a query to retrieve all objects of this type. If an attribute is defined with a uniqueness constraint (such as `bonitaBPMId` in the `VacationAvailable` object) the query returns a unique object, and not a list of objects.

You can also define a custom query to implement some logic specific to your process. For example, you can define a query that returns a list of `VacationRequest` objects for a specific user where the status of the request is either pending or approved. We will use this query to construct the user vacation statement page.

Here is a list of custom queries that will be used in the process:

- *findModifiableByBonitaBPMId* for `VacationRequest`
  Retrieves the list of vacation requests created by a specified user that can be modified. You will use this query to create a form to test the modification process.
- *findCancellableByBonitaBPMId* for `VacationRequest`
  Retrieves the list of vacation requests created by a specified user that can be cancelled. You will use this query to create a form to test the cancellation process.

There are no custom queries for `VacationAvailable`.

To create the `findModifiableByBonitaBPMId` custom query on `VacationRequest`, follow these steps:

1. From the Development menu, choose Business Data Model, then choose Manage.
2. Select the `VacationRequest` object.
3. Go to the Queries tab and select Custom.
4. Click Add.
5. Enter the name for the new query, **findModifiableByBonitaBPMId.**
6. In the query row, click in the Query column and click the (...) button.
7. By default you get a SQL query that filters on all elements (except the auto-generated persistence ID) using parameters for each of them. Edit the query code and replace it with this:

```
SELECT l
FROM VacationRequest l
WHERE l.requesterBonitaBPMId = :requesterBonitaBPMId
AND l.startDate > CURRENT_DATE
AND l.status IN('pending')
ORDER BY l.startDate ASC
```

8. In the Parameters list, you need to keep only the `requesterBonitaBPMId` parameter. Select and delete the others one by one.
9. For the Result type, select Multiple.
10. Click OK to validate your query definition.

Follow the same steps to define the `findCancellableByBonitaBPMId` query, with the following settings:

- Query:

```
SELECT l
FROM VacationRequest l
WHERE l.requesterBonitaBPMId = :requesterBonitaBPMId
AND l.status IN('pending', 'approved')
ORDER BY l.startDate ASC
```

- Parameter: `requesterBonitaBPMId` (javaLang.Long)
- Result type: Multiple

When you have defined the queries, click Finish. A warning popup is displayed to remind you of the potential impact of changing the business data model. It also contains an option to reset the model to apply any changes to unique constraints. You have defined a unique constraint, so check the Clear data option in the popup, then click OK.

Indexes

For search operations on business objects to be efficient, you can add indexes on the attributes and groups of attributes that are used to find objects. Indexes are defined for each object declared in the business data model.

On `VacationRequest` add indexes on:

- `requesterBonitaBPMId`
- `requesterBonitaBPMId, status`
- `requesterBonitaBPMId, status, startDate`

On `VacationAvailable` add an index on `bonitaBPMId`.

To add an index, follow these steps:

1. From the Development menu, choose Business Data Model, then choose Manage.
2. In the List of Business Objects, select a business object.
3. Go to the Indexes tab.
4. Click Add.
5. Enter the name for the new index. You can keep the default name.
6. In the index row, click in the Attributes column and click the (...) button.
7. In the list on the left (Available attributes) select the attributes to include in the index you are creating and then click the Add button. You can either select one attribute at a time and click Add each time, or you can hold down the Ctrl key to select multiple attributes.
8. Click OK to validate your index definition.

Repeat these steps to define all the indexes.

Initialize VacationAvailable for Employees

The `availableDays` attribute of the `VacationAvailable` object stores the number of vacation days available for each user. Each time a request is submitted, the number of days requested is deducted from the total. If the request is refused, the number of days is added back to the total. If a request is modified or cancelled, the total is adjusted as required.

The value of `availableDays` needs to be initialized for all current employees at the start of the year. It also needs to be created for any new employee who joins partway through the year. Such an operation for a new employee is typically part of a larger onboarding process.

Creating the `VacationAvailable` object for each employee and initializing `available Days` is done in a process. Creation of this process is not covered in this book, because it depends on corporate and national legislation and practice, so is different in every case. There is an example process that you can download for testing and to use as the starting point for creating your own process. To use the example process without any changes, follow these steps:

1. After referencing "Downloads" on page 9, get the *Example-InitiateVacationAvailable* process from the book's website.
2. In Bonita BPM Studio, click the Import icon on the menu bar and import the process. The process is automatically opened in the Studio.
3. Go to the Diagram menu and choose Duplicate. In the popup, change the diagram name to **Tahiti-InitiateVacationAvailable**, and then click OK. The new process is displayed. You can now close the *Example-InitiateVacationAvailable* diagram.
4. With the *Tahiti-InitiateVacationAvailable* process displayed in the whiteboard, click the Run icon in the menu bar. A form is displayed in your browser.
5. Click the "Initialize vacation available" button on the form. You can then close the browser window, and close the process in the Studio.

You can safely run the *Tahiti-InitiateVacationAvailable* process again if you add new users, or at any time to reset the data.

You have now defined the business data model for the Tahiti application.

Define Variables

Variables specify how the business data model that you defined in the previous section applies to a specific process. When you have several processes all using the same business data model, you need to choose the part of the model that is relevant for each process, and ignore the rest. Here, you are defining your first process, so everything in the model is relevant. Follow these steps:

1. Select the *New Vacation Request* pool.
2. Go to the Details panel, Data tab, Pool variables pane.
3. Find the Business variables box, and click the Add button beside it.
4. In the name field, enter the variable name, `vacationRequest`.
5. In the Business Object list, choose VacationRequest.
6. Do not configure the default value. This will be defined later.
7. Click Finish.

The variable called `vacationRequest` is now available in the pool. It can be viewed and updated by any task in the pool. It is an instance of the `VacationRequest` object. In non-Java terms, this means that it has the same structure as the `VacationRequest`.

The process also needs access to the number of days available to the requester, to decrease the number of days available when a user request is submitted. Follow the preceding steps to create a variable named `requesterVacationAvailable` that references the `VacationAvailable` object.

Specify Information Needed by a Process

In Bonita BPM, there is a clear separation between the business logic, which is contained in a process, and the user interface, which is the set of forms used in the process. To make sure that the process receives the information it needs at each stage, you use a contract. A contract is the definition of the information the process needs to start or to execute a task. You define a process contract for process instantiation and a task contract for each user task.

The *Tahiti-NewVacationRequest* process starts when a user submits a request. It creates a `vacationRequest` variable that contains values for the attributes that are relevant:

requesterBonitaBPMId
> The identity of user submitting the vacation request, which is detected automatically by the system

startDate
> The first day of vacation, specified by the requester

returnDate
> The first working day after the vacation, specified by the requester

numberOfDays
> The number of vacation days, specified by the requester

status
> The status of the request, which is automatically set to "pending" for a new request

The `reviewerBonitaBPMI` and `comments` attributes are not set, because they are only relevant after the *Review request* task.

Each item in a contract is called an input, because it is an input to the process. It is useful to use consistent names for the contract inputs and the corresponding variable attributes, but to avoid confusion between them, we use a naming convention that appends *Contract* to the name for inputs.

For *New Vacation Request*, the process contract therefore contains these inputs:

Input name	Type	Description
startDateContract	DATE	The first day of vacation.
returnDateContract	DATE	The day the requester returns to work.
numberOfDaysContract	INTEGER	The number of days of vacation, not including nonworking days.

To define the process contract, use the information from the preceding table and follow these steps:

1. Select the pool.
2. Go to the Details panel, Execution tab, Contract pane.
3. In the Inputs tab, specify the attributes required. For each one:
   a. Click Add.
   b. Specify the name of the input in the Name column.
   c. Select the Type.
   d. Add a Description. This will be displayed in the process form as a hint on how to complete the corresponding form field.
   e. Ignore the Multiple column, which is not relevant for this contract.
4. In the Constraints tab, specify the constraints on the values specified for the attributes. For each constraint, click Add and then specify a constraint name, expression, and error message. To enter an expression, click the (...) to open a popup. The error message is displayed to the user if the value specified for an attribute does not meet the constraint. These are the constraints to specify:

Name	Expression	Error message
startDateMandatory	startDateContract != null	The start date must be specified
returnDateMandatory	returnDateContract != null	The return date must be specified
returnAfterStart	returnDateContract > startDateContract	The return date must be after the start date
numberOfDaysNotZero	numberOfDaysContract >= 1	The number of days must be at least 1

Next, define the contract for the *Review request* user task. It has the following inputs:

Input	Type	Description
statusContract	TEXT	The status of the request after review: approved or refused.
commentsContract	TEXT	For a refused request, a mandatory comment explaining why the request was refused. For an approved request, a comment is optional.

The `reviewerBonitaBPMId` attribute is provided automatically and the other attributes of the `vacationRequest` are unchanged, so these do not need to be specified in the contract.

To define the contract for *Review request*, use the information from the preceding table and follow these steps:

1. Select the *Review request* task.
2. Go to the Details panel, Execution tab, Contract pane.
3. In the Inputs tab, specify the attributes required. For each one:

a. Click Add.

b. Specify the attribute in the Name column.

c. Select the Type.

d. Add a Description. This will be displayed in the process form as a hint on how to complete the corresponding form field.

4. Go to the Constraints tab. Here you specify that a comment is mandatory if the request is refused. Define the constraint as follows:

a. Click Add.

b. Specify the constraint name, `mandatoryCommentIfRefused`.

c. In the Expression column, click the (...). This opens a popup where you can specify the constraint as follows:

```
if(statusContract == "refused") {
   if(commentsContract == "") {
    return false;
   }
}

return true;
```

d. Add this Error message: *You must enter a comment for a refused request.* This message is displayed if the constraint is not met, that is, if the user refuses a vacation request but does not provide a comment.

After you have defined the contracts, you can check that the diagram and the related definitions are correct by running the process, as described in the next section.

Running the Process with Temporary Forms

You have not yet created any forms for the process, but you can run it with temporary forms that are created automatically using the contract information. The forms look incomplete because the information that is not in a contract is missing. The temporary forms are not user-friendly for application users but they are not intended for this: they are a tool for validating the contracts and process flow, and you can use them to check that the sequence of tasks is correct. The process runs as though it was started by the default user defined in the Studio Preferences, walter.bates. Walter's manager is Helen Kelly. You access the process task forms using the Bonita BPM Portal, not from the Tahiti application interface.

To test the process:

1. Select the *New Vacation Request* pool.

2. Go to the Details panel, Validation status tab, and check for any errors in the diagram. There will be information messages that no target form is defined for *New Vacation Request* or for *Review request*. This is normal. There will also be an error message on the *Request approved?* gateway, because you have not yet defined the

conditions for the outbound flows from the gateway. You can safely ignore these warnings and errors at this stage of development. You will update the process definition later with the condition information.

3. Go to the top menu bar and click Run.

4. A popup opens with a warning that some errors have been found in the diagram. Click Yes to ignore the errors and continue.

5. A new tab opens in your default browser, containing the temporary new leave request form as shown in Figure 6-3. You are automatically logged in to the Bonita BPM platform as the default user, walter.bates.

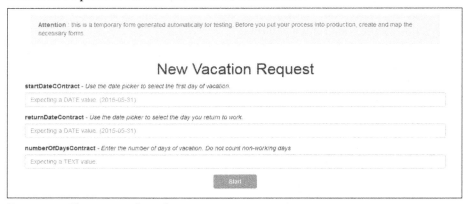

Figure 6-3. Temporary form for a new vacation request

6. Enter a value for the start date as a text string in the form *yyyy-MM-dd*, for example 2015-12-25 for December 25, 2015.

7. Enter a value for the end date using the same format as the start date.

8. Enter the number of days, and then click Start.

9. The Bonita BPM Portal is displayed, showing the task list for walter.bates.

10. At the top-right, right-click the username and choose Logout.

11. Log in as helen.kelly, with the default password bpm. Go to the Tasks view, and you will see the *Review request* task. This shows that the sequence of tasks was defined correctly.

You have verified that the process sequence is correct, so you can now continue to develop the Tahiti application.

Setting Initial Values for Variables

Business variables in your process definition are pointers to information stored in the business data database. The method for initializing a variable depends on whether it is creating new data and referencing it (for example, when creating a newRequest variable) or is referencing existing data (for example, when reading the requesterVa `cationAvailable` object). When you initialize the `newRequest` variable you are creating new data, adding it to the database, and keeping a reference. Subsequent tasks in the process use the reference to update the data, for example, with a new status value (approved, refused, or cancelled).

To initialize the `newRequest` variable with a new `VacationRequest` object instance when a request is submitted, follow these steps:

1. Select the *New Vacation Request* pool.
2. Go to the Details panel, Data tab, Pool variables pane.
3. In the Business variables box, select the variable named `vacationRequest` and click the Edit button beside it.
4. In the Default value field, click the pencil icon. This opens the expression editor.
5. Set the Type to Script.
6. Enter the script name, **createVacationRequest**.
7. Define the script return type by clicking Browse and choosing VacationRequest.
8. Enter the script content by copying this:

```
import org.bonitasoft.engine.api.ProcessAPI

import com.company.model.VacationRequest

// Create a new empty vacation request
def newVacationRequest = new VacationRequest()

// Get the id of the user who created the process instance using
// Bonita Engine API
ProcessAPI processAPI = apiAccessor.processAPI
long userId = processAPI.getProcessInstance(processInstanceId).startedBy

// Set the requester user id on the request
newVacationRequest.requesterBonitaBPMId = userId

// Update start and end date on the request
newVacationRequest.startDate = startDateContract
newVacationRequest.returnDate = returnDateContract

// Update number of days
newVacationRequest.numberOfDays = numberOfDaysContract

// Set the status to pending
newVacationRequest.status = "pending"

newVacationRequest.newRequestProcessInstanceId = processInstanceId

// Return the new object initialized
return newVacationRequest
```

9. Make sure that the "Automatic dependencies resolution" box is checked, then click OK to close the expression editor.
10. Click OK again to validate the definition.

When you initialize the `requesterVacationAvailable` variable, you get the existing value from the database. The value in the database is the number of vacation days available for the user. This value is updated every time the user submits a request for vacation days, and could also be updated by other processes.

To configure the `requesterVacationAvailable` variable to point to the number of days available for the current user, follow these steps:

1. Select the *New Vacation Request* pool.
2. Go to the Details panel, Data tab, Pool variables pane.
3. In the Business variables box, select the variable named `requesterVacationA vailable` and click Edit.
4. In the Default value field, click the pencil icon. This opens the expression editor in a popup.
5. Set the Expression type to Query.
6. In the Business Object drop-down list, select `VacationAvailable`.
7. In the Queries drop-down list, select `findByBonitaBPMId`. The query is displayed in the Query content box. You do not need to change this. However, for the query to work, you need to define a script that gets the ID of the user who initiated the process and uses it to set the value of the `bonitaBPMId` parameter.
8. In the Parameters box, click in the Value column on the right of the `bonitaBPMId` parameter.
9. Click the pencil icon. This opens another expression editor popup.
10. Set the Type to Script.
11. Enter the script name, **getInitiatorUserId**.
12. Enter the script content by copying this:

```
// Get a reference to ProcessAPI in order to retrieve process
// information
def processAPI = apiAccessor.processAPI

// Get the process instance information and return the Bonita BPM
// user id of the process initiator
return processAPI.getProcessInstance(processInstanceId).startedBy
```

13. You do not need to specify the return type because the default value is correct for this variable.
14. Click OK to close the expression editor.
15. Click OK to close the definition of the query.
16. Click OK again to validate the definition of the default value.

You have now defined the initial values for the business variables used in your process.

Updating VacationAvailable

You have already seen how to initialize VacationAvailable (in "Initialize VacationA-vailable for Employees" on page 53) for employees. This section explains how to update the *Tahiti-NewVacationRequest* process definition to adjust the number of available days in line with the users' vacation requests:

- When a vacation request is submitted, the number of days in the request must be deducted from the number of available days.
- When a vacation request is refused, the number of days in the request must be added back to the number of available days.

Open the *Tahiti-NewVacationRequest* process diagram, and follow these steps:

1. In the *Employee* lane, after the start event, add a service task. You can do this by dropping the service task icon on the flow line.
2. Go to the Details panel, General tab, General pane, and set the service task name to **Deduct requested days from available days**.
3. Go to the Details panel, Execution tab, Operations pane and define an operation to deduct the requested days from the total available.

    a. Click Add.
    b. In the lefthand box, click the down arrow and then double-click `requesterVacationAvailable`.
    c. Click "Takes value of," then in the popup choose "Use a Java method," select `setDaysAvailableCounter`, and click OK.
    d. Click the pencil icon beside the empty righthand box. This opens the expression editor.
    e. In the Expression type list, choose Script.
    f. Set the script name to **deductDays**.
    g. Enter this script:

        ```
        return requesterVacationAvailable.daysAvailableCounter -
            vacationRequest.numberOfDays
        ```

    h. Set the Return type to **java.lang.Integer**.
    i. Click OK.
4. Also in the *Employee* lane (for symmetry, but it does not really matter), add a service task on the *no* flow out of the gateway after the *Review request* task, after the *Notify employee request refused* task.
5. Set the service task name to **Credit days from refused request**.

6. Following the sames step as for the *Deduct requested days from available days* task, define an operation with a script called `creditDays` with the following content:

```
return requesterVacationAvailable.daysAvailableCounter +
vacationRequest.numberOfDays
```

You have now defined the tasks and operations in the *Tahiti-NewVacationRequest* process that will update the number of vacation days available to an employee.

Organization Data

The organization data defines the Bonita BPM users. For each user, there is a login name and password, the manager's name, and information about the groups that the user belongs to and their roles. You used this information when you ran the process to test it. Each user has a unique ID. All this information is available to all processes and process applications. You do not need to specify any variables for this. However, in the business data, you need to relate the vacation requests to users who requested and reviewed them. This is the purpose of the `requesterBonitaBPMId` and `reviewer BonitaBPMId` attributes in `VacationRequest` objects. Values are set automatically when the user submits a request and when the manager reviews it. Values will be used in application pages to construct the vacation statement for the user and the manager view.

Summary

In this chapter, you have defined the data model for the Tahiti application, and have seen your process run for the first time. In the next chapter, you will create the forms used in the *Tahiti-NewVacationRequest* process.

CHAPTER 7

Creating Process Forms

In the previous chapter, you ran your *New Vacation Request* process using temporary forms. In this chapter, you will create the forms used by the requester and reviewer in the *New Vacation Request* process.

Forms are not part of the BPMN standard. In Bonita BPM, when a process is instantiated by a user completing a form, you create a contract that defines the data that the process requires the form to return when it is submitted. You also need a contract and form for each human task.

You can use any tool to create a form, as long as the contract is respected. In this chapter, we will use the Bonita BPM Studio UI Designer. The UI Designer is an environment for creating application pages. A page is the part of an application that is visible to the user in a web browser. A page can present information to a user, and can get information from a user. A page that is part of a process is called a form.

Vacation Request Form

The vacation request form contains the set of fields that the user must complete to request vacation. This is the start date, return date, and number of days, which you specified in the data model in Chapter 6 and added to the contract for process instantiation.

To create this form there are two steps: generate the basic form, and then update it to create the form field layout that you want.

To generate the form, follow these steps:

1. Select the *New Vacation Request* pool and go to the Details panel, Execution tab, Contract pane. You will see the contract that you defined earlier.

2. Click the UI Designer icon at the right side of the Contract pane (not in the top menu bar). The UI Designer opens in your browser, with the generated form displayed in the Page Editor (see Figure 7-1).

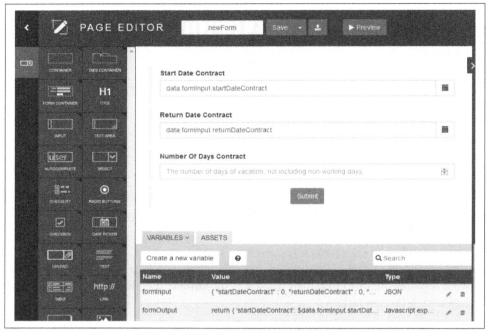

Figure 7-1. Generated vacation request form

The newly created form will work in the process, but you should update it to improve the appearance and to make it more usable.

A form consists of a set of widgets arranged on an invisible grid of rows and columns. There can be any number of rows in a page. By default there are 12 columns in a row. The palette of available widgets is in the lefthand panel, and each widget has a set of properties, shown in the righthand panel. For each input in the contract, a widget is created automatically. The widget label is the contract input name.

To update a form, you rearrange the widgets and update their properties. Follow these steps:

1. Set the form name. By default, all generated forms are called *newForm*. Double-click newForm in the top bar and enter the form name **newVacationRequestForm**.

2. In the Variables tab at the bottom of the whiteboard, on the formInput row, click the pencil icon to edit the variable and set the values of the startDateContract and returnDateContract attributes to null instead of the default value 0. Click

the Save button. By doing this, the date picker widget will open by default on today's date.

3. Hide the Variables tab and the Assets tab at the bottom of the whiteboard by clicking the down arrow in the tab label. For now, you do not need to see this information, so you can hide the tabs to have more visible space in the whiteboard.

4. Add a Title widget by dragging the Title icon from the widgets panel on the left side of the whiteboard and dropping it at the top of the whiteboard, above the Start Date Contract widget. Then go to the Properties panel on the right of the whiteboard and set the Text property to **Create a new vacation request**.

5. Select the Start Date Contract widget, go to the Properties panel and change the Label property value to **Start Date**. Then make the widget smaller, because it does not need to occupy a whole row. To do this, select the widget and change the value of the Width property. The Width property value is the number of columns that the widget occupies. Use the down arrow to reduce the value from 12 to 4.

6. Select the Number Of Days Contract widget and change the Label to **Number of Days**. Then move the widget to the same row as the Start date by selecting it and dragging it. The width will adjust automatically to use the remaining columns in the row.

7. Select the Return Date Contract widget and change the Label to **Return Date**. Then make it smaller by changing the value of the Width property to 4.

8. Click Save, and then click Preview at the top of the Page Editor. The preview shows you how the form will appear to a user, as in Figure 7-2.

Figure 7-2. Vacation request form

Manager Review Form

The manager review form displays all the information that the user entered in the request and has two fields for the manager to complete: approval and response reason. You specified these fields in the data model in Chapter 6 and added to them to the contract for the *Review request* task.

As before, there are two steps: generate the basic form from the contract, then update it.

To generate the form, follow these steps:

1. Select the *Review request* task and go to the Details panel, Execution tab, Contract pane. You will see the contract that you defined earlier.
2. Click the UI Designer icon at the right side of the Contract pane. The UI Designer opens in your browser, with the form displayed in the Page Editor (see Figure 7-3).

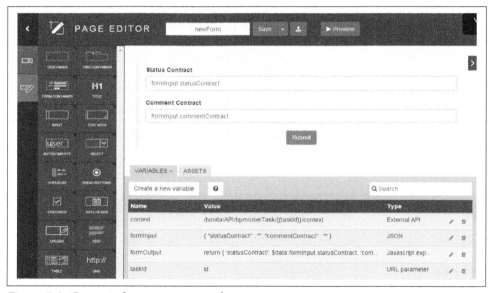

Figure 7-3. Generated vacation review form

The newly created form will work in the process, but because it contains only the items in the contract, *status* and *comment*, it is not very useful. You need to update the form to add the information from the request being reviewed, as well as to improve the form usability and appearance.

Follow these steps:

1. Set the name of the form by double-clicking newForm in the top bar and entering the form name, **reviewRequestForm**.

---

2. Add a form title by dragging a Title widget from the palette and dropping it at the top of the form. A new row is automatically inserted for the new widget. In the Text property of the title, type **Review vacation request**.
3. Add a variable that will be used to get the information from the request, as follows:
   a. Go to the Variables tab (at the bottom of the whiteboard) and click "Create a new variable."
   b. Specify the Name, `vacationRequestBusinessData`.
   c. Set the Type to **External API**.
   d. In the Value field, type `../{{context.vacationRequest_ref.link}}`
   e. Click Save.
4. Add a widget to display the start date from the request being reviewed:
   a. Drag a Date picker widget from the palette and drop it on the whiteboard.
   b. Set the Label to **Start Date**.
   c. Set the Read-only property to Yes.
   d. In the Value property enter the variable `vacationRequestBusinessData.startDate`. This is called binding the value to this variable.
5. Add a read-only Input widget labeled **Number of Days**, bound to `vacationRequestBusinessData.numberOfDays`.
6. Add a read-only Date picker widget labeled **Return Date**, bound to `vacationRequestBusinessData.returnDate`.
7. Delete the Status Contract widget that was added automatically, and replace it with a Radio buttons widget:
   a. Drag the Radio buttons widget from the widget panel to the whiteboard.
   b. Set the Label property to **Status**.
   c. Set the Available values to **approved, refused**.
   d. Bind the selected value to `formInput.statusContract`.
8. Select the Comment Contract widget and change the Label to **Comment**. Then check the value of the Placeholder property. This text is displayed in the form as a hint, and is set from the Description in the contract. Update the text if necessary.
9. Select the Submit button widget and set the "Target URL on success" property value to `/bonita`. This means that after the form is successfully submitted, the Bonita BPM Portal is displayed. This is a temporary setting: when you are ready to build the final application, you will replace this setting with the URL of the Tahiti application home page.
10. Save your form and check the Preview to make sure all the necessary fields are present.
11. Rearrange the widgets into a logical order.

When you have finished, the form preview will look something like Figure 7-4:

Figure 7-4. Vacation review form

Now if you run the process by clicking Run in the Studio menu bar, you will see the forms that you created. The review form will contain the information that you enter on the request form.

Summary

You have now completed the specification of the *New Vacation Request* process and its associated forms. In the next chapter you will refine the diagram to clarify the business logic where there are conditions, branches, and parallel flows.

CHAPTER 8

Managing Decisions

In the previous chapter, you created the forms used in the *New Vacation Request* process of the Tahiti application, and ran the process to validate the simple case of a request submission followed by the approval step.

This chapter shows you how to structure a process diagram when the business logic contains branches and joins. Branches and joins are managed in the process using gateways. Conditional branches use data: back in the first iteration of your process diagram, you added an exclusive gateway for the point where the process branches depending on whether the manager approves a vacation request. Now that the data model is defined, you can specify the condition on the flows out of this gateway. In this chapter, you will learn about the other most useful gateways, and the best practice for structuring a diagram containing gateways.

Gateway Types

The BPMN2 standard defines these types of gateway: Exclusive, Event-Based, Parallel Event-Based, Inclusive, Complex, and Parallel.

The three most useful gateways are Exclusive, Inclusive, and Parallel, and these are implemented in Bonita BPM. You can mimic the behavior of the other types of gateway by using the appropriate combination of these three.

Exclusive Gateway

An exclusive gateway is an OR decision point:

- A diverging exclusive gateway creates alternative paths. It has one inbound flow, and any number of outbound flows. Only one outbound flow is followed. One outbound flow is designated as the default, and the others have a condition defined. The outbound flow conditions are evaluated in a preset order, and the process continues along the first flow where the condition is met.

- A converging exclusive gateway merges alternative paths. It has any number of inbound flows and one outbound flow. The outbound flow is activated when the first inbound flow reaches the gateway. There is no synchronization. There is no condition on the output flow. Inbound flows that arrive subsequently trigger duplicates of subsequent tasks. If this is not what you want, you can use another exclusive gateway to direct subsequent flows to an alternate path.

Inclusive Gateway

An inclusive gateway is an AND decision point:

- A diverging inclusive gateway creates parallel paths. It has one inbound flow and any number of outbound flows. An outbound flow can have a condition. The conditions for all the outbound flows are evaluated, and the process continues along all the flows where the condition is met. You can define a default flow that is taken if no outbound flow condition is met. If there is no condition on a flow, it is always taken.
- A converging inclusive gateway merges parallel paths. It has any number of inbound flows and one outbound flow. When processing has reached the gateway along all the active inbound flows, the process continues along the outbound flow.

Parallel Gateway

A parallel gateway is a synchronization point at the start or end of multiple parallel branches:

- A diverging parallel gateway creates parallel outbound flows. There can be any number of outbound flows, and they are all followed when the gateway is activated.
- A converging parallel gateway is a synchronization point. The gateway is activated when processing on all inbound flows has arrived.

A parallel gateway can have multiple inbound flows and multiple outbound flows, making it both diverging and converging.

You must always close parallel flows with a parallel gateway.

Best Practice

To avoid problems when debugging or mainting diagrams that contain gateways, we recommend that you follow these guidelines:

- Every point where a process branches should have a matching join. This makes it clear in the diagram where the alternate or parallel flows end. It also makes execution more efficient, and makes it easier to troubleshoot errors in flow during development or in production.
- Every gateway should have a name. Use clearly related names for the corresponding branch and join gateways. For example, in the Tahiti diagram, there is a branching exclusive gateway called *Request approved?*. The corresponding join gateway could be called *request approved join*.
- You can choose not to display all the names on the diagram. Display the names of branching exclusive gateways and inclusive gateways. The others are less useful in the diagram, though essential for troubleshooting.
- Name an exclusive gateway with a question.
- Conditions on branching gateways should be coherent sets; for example, a yes or no decision. The decision could be complex, but should depend on a single idea, possibly even a single variable. For example, if a branch directs flow to an on-call support manager, you can have a set of conditions: is it a weekend, is it a public holiday, is it out of hours. These all depend on a timestamp. Avoid using sets of conditions that mix unconnected ideas.
- Always define a default outbound flow for an exclusive gateway. Always define a default outbound flow (or an outbound flow with no condition) for an inclusive gateway.

Update the Diagram

You need to make the following changes to the diagram:

- Specify operations to update the `vacationRequest` with the information submitted in the form.
- Specify the condition on the *yes* flow out of the *Request approved?* gateway, to resolve the validation error.
- Modify the *no* flow after the *Request approved?* gateway so that the notification tasks are done in parallel.
- Join the alternate flows after the *Request approved?* gateway, so that the end of the conditional flow is clear and the flow is closed.

It is easier to make the changes to flows if you start with the smallest loops and work outward.

The following sections explain how to update the diagram.

Add Operations to Update the vacationRequest

There are three attributes in the vacationRequest to update after a request is reviewed: status, comments, and reviewerBonitaBPMId. The status and comments are returned from the form in the contract. The reviewerBonitaBPMId is the ID of the person who performed the review task, so it is known to the Bonita BPM system.

You need to define operations to update the vacationRequest using the relevant information from the contract and the system. Follow these steps:

1. In the *Tahiti-NewVacationRequest* diagram, select the *Review request* task and go to the Details panel, Execution tab, Operations pane.
2. Specify the operation to update the status attribute:

    a. Click Add.

    b. In the Select target box, double-click vacationRequest.

    c. Click "Takes value of" and then from the Operator type menu choose "Use a Java method."

    d. In the list of methods, choose setStatus, and then click OK.

    e. Click the pencil icon beside the righthand box. This opens the expression editor.

    f. In the Expression type list, choose Contract input, then in the Name box select statusContract, and click OK.

3. Specify the operation to update the comments attribute:

    a. Click Add.

    b. In the Select target box, double-click vacationRequest.

    c. Click "Takes value of" and then from the Operator type menu choose "Use a Java method."

    d. In the list of methods, choose setComments, and then click OK.

    e. Click the pencil icon beside the righthand box. This opens the expression editor.

    f. In the Expression type list, choose Contract input, then in the Name box select commentsContract, and click OK.

4. Specify the operation to update the reviewerBonitaBPMId attribute:

    a. Click Add.

    b. In the Select target box, double-click vacationRequest.

    c. Click "Takes value of" and then from the Operator type menu choose "Use a Java method."

    d. In the list of methods, choose setReviewerBonitaBPMId, and then click OK.

    e. Click the pencil icon beside the righthand box. This opens the expression editor.

    f. In the Expression type list, choose Script, set the script Name to **getPerformerId**, and enter this script:

```
    return taskAssigneeId;
```

g. Make sure the Return type is set to java.lang.Long, and then click OK.

You have now defined the operations to update the attributes of the vacationRe quest. You can now define conditions that use these attributes, specifically the status of the request.

Add Flow Conditions

The *Request approved?* gateway has two outgoing flows, one for *yes* and one for *no*. The *no* flow is the default. The *yes* flow is taken if the vacation request is approved, that is, if value of the status attribute of the vacationRequest is approved.

To make the *no* flow the default:

1. Select the *no* flow out of the gateway.
2. Go to the Details panel, General tab, General pane.
3. Check the Default flow box.

To define this condition on the *yes* flow:

1. Select the *yes* flow out of the gateway.
2. Go to the Details panel, General tab, General pane.
3. Next to Condition, check Use expression.
4. Click the pencil icon next to the text field. This opens a popup where you specify the condition.
5. In the Expression type list, click Script.
6. Enter a name, **isApproved**.
7. In the center box, enter this script:

```
    return vacationRequest.status == "approved"
```

8. Click OK.

The condition is defined. To check that it is correct, go to the Details panel, Validation status tab, and click Refresh. If the condition is correctly defined, there will be no validation error listed for the gateway.

Make the no Flow Parallel

When a manager refuses a vacation request, there are several service tasks that follow: notifying the employee and HR and updating the empoylees' available vacation. All of these tasks must be completed before the flow ends, so parallel flows are needed. You need to add a diverging gateway after the *Request approved?* gateway, with one flow for each task, and then add a converging gateway to join the flows after the service tasks. There is no decision at the diverging gateway because both flows must be followed, so use a parallel gateway. Follow these steps:

1. Go to the palette and find the icon for the parallel gateway.
2. Drag the icon onto the whiteboard and drop it on the *no* flow. This automatically inserts the gateway in the flow. Call the new gateway **after refusal branch**. It is created with an outbound flow to the *Notify employee request refused* task.
3. Select the flow out of the *Notify employee request refused* task and delete it.
4. Add a flow from the *after refusal branch* gateway to the *Credit days from refused request* task.
5. Add a flow from the *after refusal branch* gateway to the *Notify HR request refused* task. You should now have three flows out of the *after refusal branch* gateway.
6. Add a second parallel gateway to the diagram. It does not matter where this gateway is, but to keep the diagram tidy, put it in the Manager lane. Call the gateway **after refusal join**, so that it is clear this is the end of the parallel flows created by the *after refusal branch* gateway.
7. Add flows from the *Credit days from refused request, Notify employee request refused,* and *Notify HR request refused* tasks to the *after refusal join* gateway.
8. Delete the flow from the *Notify HR request refused* task to *End2*.
9. Move the end icon to the *Manager* lane, beside the *after refusal join* gateway.
10. Add a flow from the *after refusal join* gateway to *End2*.
11. Hide the names of the *after refusal branch* and *after refusal join* gateways. For each gateway:
    a. Select the gateway.
    b. Go to the Details panel, Appearance tab.
    c. Uncheck the Display name box.

The flow following the refusal of a vacation request is now parallel.

Close Flows from Request approved?

In logic terms, the *Request approved?* gateway is the start of an "if" statement. The flows from the *Request approved?* gateway diverge and currently lead to two separate end points. In this section, you will add a gateway to indicate the end-if point where the alternate flows join. Follow these steps:

1. Drag the exclusive gateway icon from the palette and drop it on the flow between the *after refusal join* gateway and *End2*.
2. Name this gateway **request approved join**.
3. Delete the *End1* end point.
4. Add a flow from the *Notify employee request approved* task to the *request approved join* gateway.

5. Select the *request approved join* gateway, go to the Details panel, Appearance tab, and hide the gateway name.

The flow is now closed, and the diagram has a single end point. Change the name of the end point by selecting *End2* and specifying a new name, **New Vacation Request End**, in the Details panel, General tab, General pane. You can hide the name using the Appearance tab.

The diagram is functionally correct but not tidy. It is a good idea to rearrange the icons and flow to improve the diagram usability, to make future changes and maintenance easier.

Updated Diagram

After these updates and some tidying, the diagram looks like Figure 8-1:

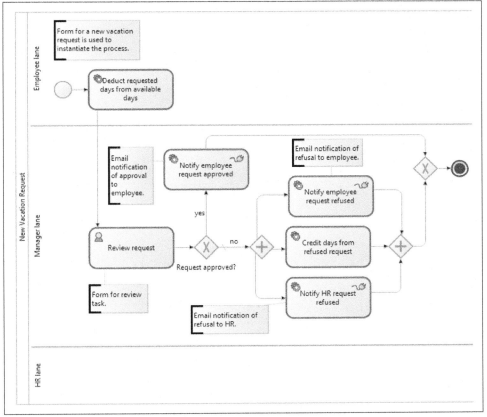

Figure 8-1. Diagram updated to close flows

Summary

You have updated the diagram to properly manage the consequences of decisions, using gateways to branch and join flows, and have defined a condition at a gateway using the data model you defined in the previous chapter. The diagram is now complete for the typical process flow.

The next chapter explains how to add checks into the process flow so that if there is a delay the task is escalated, and how to handle exceptions when something happens that you cannot plan for.

CHAPTER 9

Planning for Escalations and Exceptions

So far, this book has considered the normal use of an application, where everything works as planned. It is also necessary to consider what might not go according to plan in a process. This chapter considers the following abnormal situations:

Escalations
> Actions to advance the process flow when it is delayed

Exceptions
> Transient errors in process flow caused by temporary unavailability of external services

Escalations

It is good practice to build fail-safes into your process diagram for when the process flow gets blocked. A fail-safe is activated when some predefined condition is met or not met. There are two common types of fail-safes: reminders and escalations. A reminder is simply a message to someone that they have a task to perform. An escalation is reassigning the task to someone else.

In the Tahiti application, you will add a reminder so that if a manager does not review a vacation request within one week of submission, an automatic reminder is sent by email. You will also add an escalation, so that if there is a further delay, the vacation request can be reviewed by someone else. In the classic case, this is an escalation to the manager's manager, but to be sure that one person's absence does not block the process, you will escalate the review task to a group of people.

Add a Reminder

To add an automatic email reminder for a human task, you need to add a timer to the task. If the task has not started by the time limit, an extra flow starts, leading to a service task that will send the email reminder.

The timer is added with a noninterrupting boundary timer event. It is noninterrupting because the task still exists and is still assigned to the manager. It is a boundary event because it is positioned on the edge of a task and triggers an additional flow when the timer condition is met. The extra flow starts, but does not interrupt the normal flow.

Follow these steps:

1. Select the *Review request* task. The context menu is displayed.
2. Click the boundary event icon (below the bottom center of the highlighted task border). You will see a set of event types.
3. Click the icon for a noninterrupting timer. The timer is added to the boundary of the task. It has an error indicator, because you have not yet configured the time limit or added the extra flow (called an exception transition).
4. Add the flow to be taken if the time limit is reached. To do this:
   a. Click the timer icon on the task boundary to display the context menu.
   b. In the Details panel, General tab, rename the timer **reviewRequestTimer**, then hide the name by going to the Appearance tab and unchecking the Display name box.
   c. Drag the task icon from the context menu and drop it. This creates a service task connected to the timer.
   d. Rename the service task **Send reminder**.
   e. Select *Send reminder* to display the context menu.
   f. Drag the circle icon from the context menu and drop it. You will see a set of different circles, which represent start and end types.
   g. Choose the simple End type. This ends this flow without ending the entire process.
   h. Select the end event, and rename it **End reminder**. Then hide the name.

5. Add the time limit. This is called a timer condition. To do this:
   a. Click the timer icon on the task boundary, and go to the Details panel, General tab.
   b. Next to Timer Condition, click Edit. A popup for defining the condition opens.
   c. For "Timer condition based on," click Duration.
   d. Set the duration to seven days by clicking the up and down arrows on the Days selector until it shows 7.

e. Click "Generate duration expression." This creates the expression in the form needed by the timer, 7 Days 00:00:00. You can see this in the Timer Condition box.

f. Click Finish. This saves the timer condition.

6. In your diagram, check that the error indicator is no longer present. If you can still see it, go to the Details panel, Validation status tab, and click Refresh.

You have now added the flow for sending a reminder to the manager if a time limit is reached. The extra flow should now look like Figure 9-1:

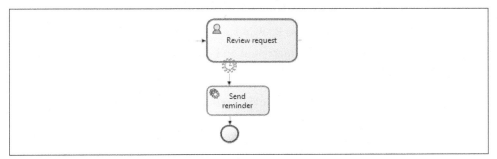

Figure 9-1. Manager review reminder flow

In Chapter 12, you will come back to this flow and configure the task to send email.

Add an Escalation

In the previous section, you added a timer that triggered an extra flow for sending a reminder to a manager who does not review vacation requests within seven days. Now you will add a replacement flow that will be activated by a timer if a vacation request is still not reviewed after the reminder is sent. In this case, the timer is an interrupting timer, so if it is triggered, you abandon the task that was automatically assigned to the manager, and replace it with a new review task that can be done by any of the people mapped to the vacationReviewerBackup actor.

Follow these steps:

1. Select the *Review request* task. The context menu is displayed.
2. Click the boundary event icon. You will see a set of event types.
3. Click the icon for a timer; the timer is added to the boundary of the task. It has an error indicator, because you have not yet configured the time limit.
4. Select the timer and configure it:

   a. Rename it **reviewRequestEscalationTimer**, and hide the name.

   b. Set the timer condition to ten days, following the procedure in the previous section. The reminder flow is activated if the request has not been reviewed after seven days. Setting a time limit of ten days for this escalation flow means that this flow will be followed if the request has still not been reviewed three days after the reminder was sent.

5. Add a lane called **ReviewerBackup lane**.

6. In this new lane, add a human task after the timer, and name it **Review request escalation**. Configure this task as follows:

    a. Specify the same form as for the *Review request* task, `reviewRequestForm`.

    b. Specify the same contract as for the *Review request* task, which you specified in "Specify Information Needed by a Process" on page 55.

    c. Specify the same operations as for the *Review request* task, which you specified in "Add Operations to Update the vacationRequest" on page 72.

7. Create the actor for the *ReviewerBackup* lane:

    a. Select the *New Vacation Request* pool and go to the Details panel, General tab, Actors pane.

    b. Click Add.

    c. Enter the actor name, **vacationReviewerBackup**.

    d. Enter a description explaining that this actor represents the people who can review vacation requests if a manager does not review them in the specified time.

    e. Do *not* click "Set as initiator."

    f. Click Finish.

8. Configure the actor for the *ReviewerBackup* lane:

    a. Select the lane and go to the Details panel, General tab, Actors pane.

    b. From the "Select an actor" drop-down list, select `vacationReviewerBackup`.

    c. Do not select an actor filter.

9. Drag the exclusive gateway icon from the palette and drop it on the link out of *Review request*. This will break the link and insert the gateway. Call the gateway **reviewRequestEscalationJoin**, and hide the name.

10. Add a flow from the *Review request escalation* task to the *reviewRequestEscalationJoin* gateway. This connects the replacement flow back to the normal flow.

This completes the changes needed in the diagram, though you might choose to make further changes to make the diagram more readable. The *Review request* task and its associated flows now looks something like Figure 9-2:

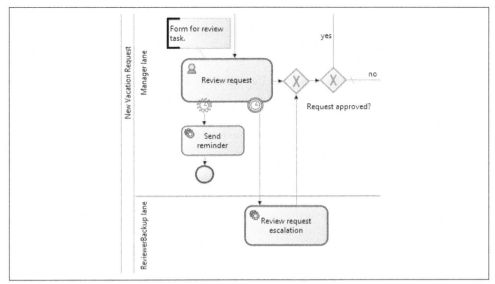

Figure 9-2. Manager review reminder and escalation flows

Now you need to specify the people in the organization who can review vacation requests that are escalated. This is not defined in the diagram but in the organization, so that it can be changed easily.

Define escalation approvers

In this section you will add a group to the example organization, and then add some people to this group. The group is the set of people who can review vacation requests when there is an escalation because the requester's manager does not review the request within the time limit. As an example, we will include in the group all of the managers in the ACME organization. There are the following managers:

- Daniela Angelo
- Favio Riviera
- Helen Kelly
- Michael Morrison
- William Jobs
- Zachary Williamson

Follow these steps:

1. Go to the Organization menu and choose Manage. This opens the Manage organizations dialog, with a list of organizations. The example organization in Bonita BPM Studio is called ACME, and it should be marked active.

2. Select ACME and click Next. The group hierarchy is displayed. The default groups represent a typical corporate structure, with a group defined for each department, but groups can be created based on any criteria, and users can belong to many groups.

3. Click Add group. The Details fields become active. Specify the group:

   a. Specify a group name, **vacationReviewers**. The group name is used to create the path, so must not contain spaces or special characters.

   b. Specify a display name, **Vacation Reviewers**. This is the "human readable" name of the group.

   c. Add a description; for example: *This group contains the people who can review vacation requests that are escalated because they are not reviewed by the requester's manager within the normal time limit.*

4. Click Next. The roles page is displayed.

5. Click Next. The list of users is displayed.

6. Add the users listed earlier to the `vacationReviewers` group. For each user:

   a. Select the user by clicking on the line in the list.

   b. Go to the Membership tab.

   c. Click Add membership.

   d. From the Group drop-down list, choose `/vacationReviewers`.

   e. From the Role drop-down list, choose member.

7. Click Finish. This saves the updated organization definition, with the `vacationReviewers` group and its members. A popup for publishing the modification opens. Click Yes.

When you are ready to run the process, map the `vacationReviewerBackup` actor to the `vacationReviewers` group. You can change the members of this group, even after the process is in production, without having to change the process diagram. To map the actor to the group, follow these steps:

1. Click the Configure icon in the menu bar. The configuration dialog opens at the Actor mapping view.

2. In the Actor mapping box in the center, select `vacationReviewerBackup`.

3. Click Groups. The list of groups in the organization is displayed.

4. Check the box beside the `/vacationReviewers` group, and then click Finish.

5. Click Finish to close the configuration dialog.

The actor mapping is now defined, so you can run the process.

Exceptions

An exception is an error that prevents the application from running successfully. Typically, exceptions are caused by transient problems with your environment. For example, a network outage means that your application cannot connect to your email service. When the network outage is over, the application will run normally. Any tasks that failed because of the outage can be recovered by the administrator. The administrator uses Bonita BPM Portal to check the status of tasks and process instances (called *Cases* in the Portal). The precise recovery steps required in the Portal depend on the exception and are outside the scope of this book.

Other exceptions could indicate errors in your application or process, or a bug in the underlying software. However, these should be detected and fixed during application testing.

Summary

In this chapter, you have updated the *Tahiti-NewVacationRequest* process diagram to add automatic reminders and escalations for review tasks, including placeholders for the connections to email systems.

In the next chapter, you will convert the application prototype that you created in "Create the Application Prototype" on page 15 into a real application that uses this process.

CHAPTER 10

Building the Application

In the previous chapter, you updated the process definition for a new vacation request to add escalations. The Tahiti application definition does not yet meet all the requirements described in "Example Application: Vacation Management" on page 7, but it is complete enough that you can build and test a first version.

This chapter explains how to convert the Tahiti application page prototype into the real page that uses real data. Then you can build the Tahiti application with links from the application page to the relevant process tasks.

These are the stages in building the application:

1. Deploy and run the related processes.
2. Update the vacation statement page to use real business and organization data instead of the dummy variables that you defined in the prototype.
3. Create the application definition.
4. Test the application as a user and as a manager.

You will carry out these stages in the development environment and validate the application.

Deploy and Run Processes

In the development environment, you deploy a process by running it from Bonita BPM Studio. You can check that the process is deployed and is operating correctly by running it from the Bonita BPM Portal.

To deploy and check the *Tahiti-NewVacationRequest* process, follow these steps:

1. Open the *Tahiti-NewVacationRequest* process. Select it and click Run. This deploys the process. You can ignore the form that is displayed.

2. Open and run the *Tahiti-InitiateVacationAvailable* process. This initializes the data used in the application. Click the button in the form that is displayed to initialize the data.
3. Open the Bonita BPM Portal by clicking the Portal icon in the Studio menu bar. You will be logged in as the user defined in your Studio Preferences server settings. By default, this is Walter Bates.
4. At the top-right of the Portal page, click the down arrow beside User and choose Administrator from the drop-down list. This sets the current profile to Administrator.
5. Go to the BPM menu and choose Processes. In the list of processes, you will see the *Tahiti-NewVacationRequest* and *Tahiti-InitiateVacationAvailable* processes that you have deployed.

The new vacation request process is now ready to be called from the application page.

Update the Vacation Statement

In "Create the Application Prototype" on page 15 you created a prototype of the vacation statement application page. This section explains how to create the real application page. For now this will not include active buttons to modify or cancel a vacation request, because you have not yet defined the processes to handle those options.

Follow these steps:

1. In the UI Designer, open the application page prototype, *TahitiVacationManagement*.
2. Select the "Cancel selected vacation" button and set the Disabled property to yes. You have not yet created the process to handle cancellation of a vacation request.
3. Disable the "Modify selected vacation" button in the same way.
4. Add a new External API variable called `session` with the following value: `../API/system/session/1`
5. Select the username Text widget at the top-right of the page, and change the Text property to `{{session.user_name}}`.
6. Add a new External API variable called `processCreate` with the following value: `../API/bpm/process?s=New Vacation Request&p=0&c=10&o=version&f=activationState=ENABLED`.
7. Add a new JavaScript expression variable called `urlStartCreateProcess` with the following value:

```
// Return the URL to the new vacation request process
// instantiation form
if ($data.processCreate &&
    $data.processCreate.length > 0) {
  return "/bonita/portal/resource/process/" +
    $data.processCreate[$data.processCreate.length-1].name +
```

```
            "/"+$data.processCreate[$data.processCreate.length-1].version +
            "/content/?id=" +
            $data.processCreate[$data.processCreate.length-1].id;
    } else {
      return null;
    }
```

8. Edit the definitions of the variables:

   - myVacation: change the type to External API and set the value to:
     `../API/bdm/businessData/com.company.model.VacationRequest?q=find`
     `ByRequesterBonitaBPMId&p=0&c=100&f=requesterBonitaBPMId={{ses`
     `sion.user_id}}`
   - myVacationAvailable: change the type to *External API*, with the following
     value: `../API/bdm/businessData/com.company.model.VacationAvailable?`
     `q=findByBonitaBPMId&p=0&c=1&f=bonitaBPMId={{session.user_id}}`
   - managerTeamInfo: change the type to *External API*, with the following
     value: `../API/extension/vacationRequest`

   These variables are already used in the relevant widgets, so you do not need to
   change the widget Value properties.

   The `selectedRow`, `teamSelectedRow`, `copySelectedRow`, and `hideCancel` variables do not need to be changed.

   The `managerTeamInfo` variable contains a combination of business data and
   organization data, which is retrieved using the REST API extension that you have
   downloaded. The extension needs to be deployed, as described in the next section.

9. Bind the Target URL property of the *Create new vacation request* Link widget to
   the variable `urlStartCreateProcess`: click the icon and type the variable name.

10. In the Team vacation container, Vacation requests tab, bind the Target URL prop-
    erty of the *Review selected vacation request* Link widget to the following value:
    `'/bonita/portal/form/taskInstance/' + teamSelectedRow.taskId`

11. Replace the placeholder Text widget that contains the text IMAGE with a real
    image, as follows:

    a. Go to the Assets panel below the whiteboard and click "Add a new asset." This
       opens a popup.
    b. In the popup, set the Type to Image, Source to Local, and upload the file con-
       taining the image that you want to display. Then click Add.
    c. Delete the Text widget and add an Image widget in its place.
    d. Set the Width property to 2.
    e. Set the Source Type property to Asset.
    f. Set the Asset Name property to the name of the image file that you uploaded.

g. Set the Alternate text property to the text to display if the image is not shown.

12. Preview the *Tahiti Vacation Management* page to check that there are no errors. You will see data in some of the widgets but not all. This is normal when the application processes are not running.

13. Export the page using the Export button located next to the Save button. This will create a file called *page-Tahiti Vacation Management.zip*.

Create the Application

An application consists of pages, navigation, and processes.

Before you begin, if you have not already done so, export the page from the UI Designer as you did in the previous section, and deploy the processes as you did earlier in the chapter. If you are creating an application for a deployment in a production system, you need to build the processes in Bonita BPM Studio and export them as a *.bar* file for deployment. In this chapter, however, you are creating a test application in development, so you can deploy the processes by running them from the Studio.

 By default, when you exit from Bonita BPM Studio, the Bonita BPM database is reset and you lose any resource and application definitions. To avoid this, go to the Studio Preferences Database section and uncheck all the options. This only applies to the development environment when you start the Portal and the Bonita BPM platform from the Studio.

To create the Tahiti application, follow these steps:

1. Log in to Bonita BPM Portal as a user with the Administrator profile.
2. Deploy the application page:
   a. Go to the Resources screen.
   b. Click Add. This opens the Add resource popup.
   c. In the popup, specify the *page-Tahiti Vacation Management.zip* file that you exported earlier, and then click Next.
   d. In the confirmation popup, click Confirm. The page will be imported.
   e. Check that the page is now in the Resources list. If the resource list is long, click Pages on the left to show only the page resources and hide the others.
3. Deploy the Tahiti REST API extension that you downloaded (see "Downloads" on page 9), as follows:

   a. In the Resources screen, click Add. This opens the Add resource popup.
   b. In the popup, specify the *tahiti_rest_api_extension.zip* file, and then click Next.

c. In the confirmation popup, click Confirm. The REST API extension will be imported.
4. Go to the Applications screen.
5. Click New to create a new application. This opens a dialog.
6. Enter a Display name (for example, **Tahiti Vacation Management**). This is shown in the main menu bar of the application.
7. Specify a URL. This will be used to access the application. All application URLs start with `../apps/`, so you just need to specify the unique part, for example `tahiti`.
8. Specify a Version number. This is useful when you are updating an application and need to track releases.
9. Specify the Profile of a user who can access the application. For the Tahiti application, this is User.
10. Optionally (but recommended), add a Description of the application.
11. Click Create. The application is added to the Application list.
12. Click the URL in the list to check it is created correctly. It should take you to a page with the display name in the top bar and some default content.

You have now created the Tahiti application. If you need to change any of this information, click the edit icon for the application in the application list then click More.

The next step after creating the application is to add the page. Follow these steps:

1. In the application list, click the edit icon for the Tahiti application.
2. In the Pages zone, click Add. The Add page popup opens.
3. Click in the Page field to open the list of available pages. All the page names start `custompage_`.
4. Choose `custompage_TahitiVacationManagement`.
5. In the URL field, the start of the URL, `../apps/tahiti/`, is already displayed. Enter a unique term to identify the page in the application. The Tahiti application only has this page so you can call it `index`.
6. Click Add. The Tahiti page is now listed in the Pages zone.
7. In the Tahiti index page row, point your mouse below the home page icon. A hidden control, "Set as Home page," is displayed. Click this control to make the Tahiti page the home page for the application.
8. Delete the default application home page by clicking the trashcan icon.
9. There is only one page in the Tahiti application so you do not need to define any navigation.
10. Click Back to go back to the application list. Click the URL of the Tahiti application. You will now see the Tahiti page.
11. Bookmark the Tahiti application home page in your browser.

You have created the application and defined its content. The next section explains how to test it.

Test the Application

In the previous section, you created the Tahiti vacation management application. You have done some testing along the way to make sure that the individual components work, but now it's time to test the whole application. This section outlines a test scenario that will validate almost every aspect of the application and the processes it contains.

There are three users in this scenario:

- Helen Kelly (helen.kelly), the Human Resources manager
- April Sanchez (april.sanchez), a compensation specialist who reports to Helen
- Walter Bates (walter.bates), an HR benefits specialist who also reports to Helen

April and Walter are not managers. All three users have the same password, bpm.

In this scenario, you need to use the Tahiti application as each user in turn, so you log in and log out several times using Bonita BPM Portal. In a production system, you would probably access the application from your corporate intranet, which would handle the login and you would not use Bonita BPM Portal.

The three users log in to the Portal with the User profile, and then access the Tahiti application using the browser bookmark that you created earlier. Each user has ten days of vacation available. To simplify checking, create all vacation requests for one day.

Follow these steps:

1. From Bonita BPM Studio, run the *Tahiti-InitiateVacationAvailable* process and click the button to initialize the vacation data.
2. Also in the Studio, open the *Tahiti-NewVacationRequest* process. Select it and click Run. This deploys the process. Ignore the form that is displayed.
3. Open the Bonita BPM Portal by clicking the Portal icon in the Studio menu bar. This opens the Portal and logs you in as the default user. Click the arrow beside the user's name and choose Logout.
4. Log in to the Portal as April (april.sanchez/bpm) and then open the book-marked Tahiti page in your browser.
5. As April, create two vacation requests.
6. Repeat the logout and login sequence to log in as Walter and then create two vacation requests.
7. Finally, log in as Helen and then:
   a. Create a vacation request.
   b. View the list of pending requests from the team.
   c. Select one of April's requests and refuse it, giving a reason.
   d. Select one of Walter's requests and approve it.

At the end of these steps, Helen's vacation statement should show that she has 9 days available with one pending request, April has 9 days available with one pending request, and Walter has 8 days available with one pending request.

Summary

You have created the Tahiti vacation management application for submitting and approving new vacation requests, and validated that it works correctly in the development environment. The next chapter explains how to create the processes for modifying and cancelling a request, and how to update the application to include these options.

CHAPTER 11

Managing Interruptions

An interruption is a human intervention to change the normal flow of a business process. The Tahiti application needs to handle modification or cancellation of a vacation request. These are interruptions triggered by an employee. You will enable a user to modify a pending vacation request, and to cancel a pending or approved vacation request. The user's manager must approve cancellation of a request that has already been approved. If a user wants to modify an approved request, they can cancel the approved one and submit a new request. This chapter explains how to extend the Tahiti application so that employees can modify a pending vacation request, or cancel a request.

Modify a Request

A user can modify a pending vacation request. In the Tahiti application prototype page that you have created, when the user selects a pending vacation request, a button marked Modify Vacation Request appears, together with fields to change the dates and duration of the vacation request. A user can only change a pending request, so there is no manager review step.

In this section, you will:

1. Update the Tahiti vacation management application page so that the user can change the details of a pending request in the page, then submit the change.
2. Create a new process definition, *Tahiti-ModifyPendingVacationRequest*, which is launched when the user submits an update to a request.

Add Modify Option to the Application Page

This section explains how to add fields to the Tahiti application page that the user can use to modify a pending vacation request. The user modifies the vacation request in the application page, then clicks a button to submit the change. There is no need for a separate form for updating the request. It is more efficient for the user to make the change directly in the application page.

Follow these steps:

1. Open the *TahitiVacationManagement* page in the UI Designer.
2. Create an External URL variable called `processModify` with the following value:
   `../API/bpm/process?s=Modify Pending Vacation Request &p=0&c=10&o=version&f=activationState=ENABLED`
3. Create a JavaScript expression variable called `urlStartModifyProcess` with the following value:

```
// Return the API URL to instantiate the modify vacation request
// process
if ($data.processModify  && $data.processModify.length > 0) {
  return "../API/bpm/process/" +
    $data.processModify[$data.processModify.length-1].id +
    "/instantiation";
} else {
  return null;
}
```

4. Add a Text widget with the following properties:

Text	To modify the selected vacation request, update the details in the selected request line, and then click Modify selected vacation.
Hidden	Bind to selectedRow.copy.status!=="pending"

5. Move the "Modify selected vacation" button into a row beside the Text widget that you have just added, and update the following properties:

Disabled	no
Action	POST
URL to call	{{urlStartModifyProcess}}
Data sent on click	Bind to {"vacationRequestIdContract": selectedRow.copy.persistenceId_string, "startDateContract": selectedRow.copy.startDate, "returnDateContract": selectedRow.copy.returnDate,"numberOfDaysContract":selectedRow.copy.numberOfDays}
Target URL on success	/bonita/apps/tahiti/index/

6. Add an Input widget with the following properties:

CSS classes	visibility: hidden
Value	Bind to urlStartModifyProcess

To modify a request, the user selects the request in the table. The information in the selected row is copied to the Start date, Return date, and Number of days widgets. If the status of the selected request is Pending, the "Modify selected vacation" button appears. The user updates the dates and number of days, then clicks the button. Clicking the button triggers an API call that starts an instance of the process to modify the vacation request. The next section explains how to define this process.

Create the Tahiti-ModifyPendingVacationRequest Process

To create the process that enables users to modify a vacation request, you need to do the following:

- Create the diagram to specify the process flow and tasks
- Specify the contract that defines what information the process requires
- Specify the variables used in the process
- Specify the operations that are used to update these variables and the vacation business data

Create the diagram

Create a new diagram called *Tahiti-ModifyPendingVacationRequest*. Name the pool *Modify Pending Vacation Request*. The pool needs to contain an *Employee* lane, which is created by default. In this lane, add:

- A start event
- Service tasks named

  — *Find vacation available*
  — *Update vacation available*
  — *Update vacation request*

- An end event

Your diagram should look something like Figure 11-1.

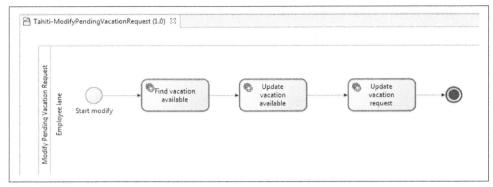

Figure 11-1. Process for modifying a vacation request

There is no need for a review step, because the pending request is already the subject of an instance of the process to review a new vacation request. When the manager reviews the request, she will see the updated information. You do not need to create an instantiation form because the process is started by an API call that provides all the data that is needed.

When you view the validation status, there are warnings about forms that are not defined. To remove the flag warning that no instantiation form is defined, select the pool, go to the Details panel, Execution tab, Instantiation form pane, and check "No form." You can do the same to remove the warning that no Overview page is defined.

Specify the contract

For *Modify Pending Vacation Request*, the process contract contains these inputs:

Input name	Type	Description
vacationRequestIdContract	TEXT	The ID of the edited vacation request.
startDateContract	DATE	The new value for the first day of vacation.
returnDateContract	DATE	The new value for the day the requester returns to work.
numberOfDaysContract	INTEGER	The new value for the number of days of vacation, not including nonworking days.

1. Select the pool.
2. Go to the Details panel, Execution tab, Contract pane.
3. In the Inputs tab, specify the attributes required. For each one:
   a. Click Add.
   b. Specify the name of the input in the Name column.
   c. Select the Type.
   d. Add a Description.

e. Ignore the Multiple column, which is not relevant for this contract.

Specify the variables

1. Select the pool and go to the Details panel, Data tab, Pool variables pane.
2. Add a business variable, vacationRequest, as follows:
   a. Beside the Business data list, which is empty, click Add. The New variable popup opens.
   b. Enter the variable name, **vacationRequest**.
   c. Set the Business Object to VacationRequest.
   d. In the Default value field, click the pencil icon. This opens the expression editor in a popup.
   e. Set the Expression type to Query.
   f. In the Business Object drop-down list, select VacationRequest.
   g. In the Queries drop-down list, select findByPersistenceId. The query is displayed in the Query content box. You do not need to change this. However, for the query to work, you need to define a script that converts the ID from a String (the type used by the contract) to a Long (the type needed for the search query parameter). Do this as follows:
      i. In the Parameters box, click in the Value column on the right of the persistenceId parameter.
      ii. Click the pencil icon. This opens another expression editor popup.
      iii. Set the Type to Script.
      iv. Enter the script name, **stringToLong**.
      v. Enter the script content by copying this:

      ```
      return Long.valueOf(vacationRequestIdContract)
      ```

      vi. You do not need to specify the return type because the default value is correct for this variable.
      vii. Click OK to close the expression editor.
   h. Click OK to close the definition of the query.
   i. Click OK again to validate the definition of the default value, and then click Finish to save the definition of the variable.
3. Add a business variable, vacationAvailable, as follows:
   a. Beside the Business data list, click Add. The New variable popup opens.
   b. Enter the variable name, **vacationAvailable**.
   c. Set the Business Object to VacationAvailable.
   d. Leave the Default value field empty.
   e. Click Finish.
4. Add the process variables numberOfDays (Integer), startDate (Date), and returnDate (Date) as follows:

a. Beside the Process variables list, click Add. The New variable popup opens.

b. Enter the variable name.

c. Set the type.

d. Set the Default value using the drop-down list to the matching contract input.

e. Click Finish & Add to add the next variable, or Finish when you have added the three variables.

Operations

Now you need to define operations to update the counter of available days for the requester and to update the pending request:

1. Select the *Find vacation available* step, go to the **Details** panel, Execution tab, Operations pane and define an operation to initialize the `vacationAvailable` business variable:

   a. Click Add.

   b. In the lefthand box, click the down arrow and then double-click `vacationAvailable`.

   c. Click the pencil icon beside the empty righthand box. This opens the expression editor.

   d. In the Expression type list, choose Query.

   e. In Business Object drop-down list select `VacationAvailable`.

   f. In the Queries drop-down list, select `findByBonitaBPMId`. The query is displayed in the Query content box.

   g. In the Parameters box, click in the Value column on the right of the `persistenceId` parameter.

   h. Click the pencil icon. This opens another expression editor popup.

   i. Set the Type to Java.

   j. In the Name box, select `vacationRequest`.

   k. In the "Browse your Java object" box, select `VacationRequest - getRequesterBonitaBPMId`.

   l. You do not need to specify the return type because the default value is correct for this variable.

   m. Click OK to close the expression editor.

   n. Click OK to close the definition of the query.

2. Select the *Update vacation available* step, go to the Details panel, Execution tab, Operations pane and define an operation to update the `daysAvailableCounter` according to the modification made by the requester:

   a. Click Add.

   b. In the lefthand box, click the down arrow and then select `vacationAvailable`.

c. Click "Takes value of," then in the popup choose "Use a Java method," select setDaysAvailableCounter, and click OK.

d. Click the pencil icon beside the empty righthand box. This opens the expression editor.

e. In the Expression type list, choose Script.

f. Set the script name to **calculateNewDaysAvailableCounter**.

g. Enter this script:

```
vacationAvailable.daysAvailableCounter +
vacationRequest.numberOfDays - numberOfDays
```

h. Set the Return type to **java.lang.Integer**.

i. Click OK.

3. Select the *Update vacation request* step, go to the Details panel, Execution tab, Operations pane and define an operation that uses the value of the process variable that stores the modification made by the requester to update the numberOf Days:

a. Click Add.

b. In the lefthand box, click the down arrow and then double-click vacationRe quest.

c. Click "Takes value of," then in the popup choose "Use a Java method," select setNumberOfDays, and click OK.

d. In the righthand box, click the down arrow and then select numberOfDays.

4. Repeat the previous step to define an operation to update the startDate and an operation to update the returnDate.

This completes the definition of the process to modify a pending vacation request.

Cancel a Request

When a user cancels a vacation request before it is approved, the process that was previously started to approve the request must be stopped. If the request is already approved, the manager needs to approve the cancellation, in case the employee is not using up vacation days correctly.

The starting point for cancelling a vacation request is the vacation statement that you created in "Create the Application Prototype" on page 15 and updated in the previous section to enable pending requests to be modified. The employee selects a vacation request in the table and clicks the Cancel button, which starts the cancellation process.

In this section, you will:

1. Update the Tahiti vacation management application page so that the user can request cancellation of a pending or approved request in the home page.

2. Create a new process definition, *Tahiti-CancelVacationRequest*, which is launched when the user submits a cancellation request.
3. Modify the *Tahiti-NewVacationRequest* process to handle cancellation of a pending request.
4. Create the form used by a manager to review a cancellation request and approve or refuse it.

Add a Cancel Option to the Application Page

This section explains how to add a button to the Tahiti application page that the user can use to cancel a vacation request. A request can be cancelled if it is pending or approved. The user selects the vacation request in the application page, then clicks a button to submit the cancellation request. There is no need for a separate cancellation form. It is more efficient for the user to make the change directly in the application page.

A request that is pending is cancelled immediately when the user clicks the Cancel button. For an approved request, manager approval is needed, so the vacation request goes into a special state, processing cancellation, until the cancellation is approved or refused.

To update the application page, follow these steps:

1. Open the *TahitiVacationManagement* page in the UI Designer.
2. Create a new External API variable called `processCancel`, with the following value: `../API/bpm/process?s=Cancel Vacation Request&p=0&c=10&o=version&f=activationState=ENABLED`
3. Create a new JavaScript expression variable called `urlStartCancelProcess`, with the following value:

```
// Return the API URL to instantiate the cancel vacation request
// process
if ($data.processCancel  && $data.processCancel.length > 0) {
  return "../API/bpm/process/" +
    $data.processCancel[$data.processCancel.length-1].id +
    "/instantiation";
} else {
  return null;
}
```

4. Add a Text widget with the following properties:

Text	To cancel the selected vacation request, click Cancel selected vacation. If the request is already approved, a cancellation request will be sent to your manager.
Hidden	Bind to !(selectedRow.copy && selectedRow.copy.status!=="refused")

5. Move the "Cancel selected vacation" button into a row beside the Text widget that you have just added, and set the following properties:

Disabled	no
Action	POST
URL to call	{{urlStartCancelProcess}}
Data sent on click	Bind to {"vacationRequestIdContract": selectedRow.copy.persistenceId_string}
Target URL on success	/bonita/apps/tahiti/index/

6. Add an Input widget with the following properties:

CSS classes	visibility: hidden
Value	Bind to urlStartCancelProcess

You now have the final version of the Tahiti application page. Export it by clicking the Export icon in the top bar. This creates a *.zip* archive that you will deploy later, in "Update the Application" on page 132.

Define the Tahiti-CancelVacationRequest Process

You need to define a process to handle the cancellation request. It checks whether the request to be cancelled is pending or approved. If it is approved, it presents the manager with a form to review the cancellation. If the request is pending, it sends a message to the active *New Vacation Request* process to cancel the request. You need to update the *New Vacation Request* process to receive the message and take the actions needed to cancel the request.

To create the cancellation process, you need to do the following:

- Create the diagram for the new process
- Specify the variables used in the process
- Specify the actors for the lanes
- Configure the communication between the new process and the *New Vacation Request* process
- Define conditions that determine the correct flow
- Update the status of the vacation request
- Update the number of available vacation days for the user when a request is cancelled

The following sections explain how to do this.

Create the diagram

1. Create a new diagram called *Tahiti-CancelVacationRequest*.
2. Rename the pool **Cancel Vacation Request**.
3. The *Employee lane* is added by default, so you do not need to change it. Add a lane called **Manager lane**.
4. Create the process flow shown in Figure 11-2. There is a human task where the manager reviews the cancellation request, and there are several service tasks where data is updated. There is one new diagram element that you have not seen before, a throw message event. The error indicators are reminders to complete the configuration, which you will do this later in this chapter.

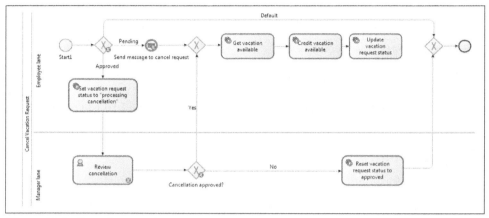

Figure 11-2. Cancel a vacation request

Specify the contract

For *Cancel Vacation Request*, the process contract contains only one input, *vacation-RequestIdContract*. To define the contract:

1. Select the pool and go to the Details panel, Execution tab, Contract pane.
2. Click Add.
3. Specify the name of the input, **vacationRequestIdContract**, in the Name column.
4. Leave the Type set to the default value, text.
5. Add a Description: *The id of the vacation request to be cancelled.* This will be displayed in the process form as a hint on how to complete the corresponding form field.
6. Ignore the Multiple column, which is not relevant for this contract. For review cancellation, the step contract contains one input, cancellationApprovedContract. To define the contract:

a. Select the Review cancellation step and go to the Details panel, Execution tab, Contract pane.

b. Click Add.

c. Specify the name of the input, `cancellationApprovedContract`, in the Name column.

d. Set the Type to Boolean.

e. Add a Description: The manager decision about vacation request cancellation.

f. Ignore the Multiple column, which is not relevant for this contract.

Specify the variables

1. Select the pool and go to the Details panel, Data tab, Pool variables pane.

2. Add a process variable, `cancellationApproved`, as follows:

   a. Beside the Process data list, which is empty, click Add. The New variable popup opens.

   b. Enter the variable name, **cancellationApproved**.

   c. Set the type to Boolean.

   d. Click Finish.

3. Add a business variable, `vacationRequestToCancel`, as follows:

   a. Beside the Business data list, which is empty, click Add. The New variable popup opens.

   b. Enter the variable name, **vacationRequestToCancel**.

   c. Set the Business Object to `VacationRequest`.

   d. In the Default value field, click the pencil icon. This opens the expression editor in a popup.

   e. Set the Expression type to Query.

   f. In the Business Object drop-down list, select `VacationRequest`.

   g. In the Queries drop-down list, select `findByPersistenceId`. The query is displayed in the Query content box. You do not need to change this. However, for the query to work, you need to define a script that converts the ID from a String (the type used by the contract) to a Long (the type needed for the search query parameter). Do this as follows:

      i. In the Parameters box, click in the Value column on the right of the `persistenceId` parameter.

      ii. Click the pencil icon. This opens another expression editor popup.

      iii. Set the Type to Script.

      iv. Enter the script name, **stringToLong**.

      v. Enter the script content by copying this:

      ```
      return Long.valueOf(vacationRequestIdContract)
      ```

     vi. You do not need to specify the return type because the default value is correct for this variable.

    vii. Click OK to close the expression editor.

  h. Click Finish.

  i. Click OK to close the definition of the query.

  j. Click OK again to validate the definition of the default value, and then click Finish to save the definition of the variable.

4. Add a business variable, `requesterVacationAvailable`, as follows:

  a. Beside the Business data list, click Add. The New variable popup opens.

  b. Enter the variable name, **requesterVacationAvailable**.

  c. Set the Business Object to `VacationAvailable`.

  d. Click Finish.

Now specify how the `cancellationApproved` variable is updated with the manager's decision. This is done with an operation on the Review cancellation human task, as follows:

1. Select the Review cancellation task go to the Details panel, Execution tab, Operations pane, and click Add.
2. In the Select target box, double-click `cancellationApproved`.
3. Leave the operation type set to the default, "Takes value of."
4. In the righthand box, double-click `cancellationApprovedContract`.

Configure actors

An actor defines who can carry out the tasks in a lane. For the *Employee* lane, the Employee actor is specified by default so you do not need to do anything. For the *Manager* lane, configure an actor and actor filter as follows:

1. Select the *Manager* lane and go to the Details panel, General tab, Actors pane.
2. In the "Select an actor" drop-down list, select the Employee actor.
3. Select the *Review cancellation* task, and then click Set beside "Actor filter."
4. In the popup, select "Initiator manager," and then click Next.
5. Enter a name for this actor filter, **cancellationRequesterManager**, then click **Next**.
6. Make sure that the "Assign task automatically" box is checked, and then click Finish.

Configure the communication between the processes

Configure the *Send message to cancel request* throw message event. This event sends a message to the *New Vacation Request* process that is in progress for the vacation request that the user wants to cancel. Follow these steps:

1. Select the throw message event, *Send message to cancel request*.
2. Go to the Details panel, General tab, Messages pane.
3. Click Add. The Add message popup opens.
4. Enter a name, **cancellationMessage**.
5. Enter a description: **Message to cancel a vacation request**.
6. Specify the Target pool by double-clicking "New Vacation Request" from the dropdown list.
7. Specify the Target element by typing **Catch cancellation message**. You will add the catch message event to the *Tahiti-NewVacationRequest* later in this chapter.
8. Go to the "Correlation between instances" tab. A correlation key guarantees that the message is sent to the correct instance of the other process.
9. Check the "Use key-based correlation" box.
10. Click Add.
11. In the Correlation key field, type `requestId`.
12. In the Correlation value field, click the pencil icon. This opens the expression editor.
13. In Expression type choose Java, in the Name box select `vacationRequestToCancel`, and in "Browse your Java object" select `VacationRequest getPersistenceId`.
14. Click OK.
15. Click Finish.

Define flow conditions

This section explains how to set flow conditions on the gateways in the *Tahiti-CancelVacationRequest* process diagram:

1. Set conditions on the outbound flows of the *Status of request* gateway:
   a. Select the *Pending* flow, go to the Details panel, General tab, General pane, and select "Use expression." Click the pencil icon to open the expression editor. Create a Script expression called `isRequestStatusPending` with the following content:

   ```
   return vacationRequestToCancel.status == "pending"
   ```

   b. Select the *Approved* flow and click "Use expression." Click the pencil icon to open the expression editor. Create a Script expression called `isRequestStatusApproved` with the following content:

   ```
   return vacationRequestToCancel.status == "approved"
   ```

   c. Select the other flow, and configure it to be the default (check the Default flow box). This will catch any requests with a status that is neither Pending nor Approved, reducing the risk of errors, or of duplicating a cancellation request.

2. Set conditions on the outbound flows of the *Cancellation approved?* gateway:
   a. Select the *Yes* flow and click "Use expression." In the drop-down list, select the `cancellationApproved` variable.
   b. Select the *No* outbound flow and make it the default.
3. Check that the conditions are correctly set by going to the Validation status tab and clicking Refresh. The error indicators should be removed from the diagram.
4. Optionally, hide the labels on flows, to make the diagram easier to read.

Update the status of the vacation request

When a cancellation request for an approved vacation request is being processed, there are the following changes to the vacation request status:

- For any vacation requests that the user wants to cancel, the status is set to *processing cancellation* to indicate that a cancellation is in progress.
- If cancellation is refused, the status is set back to *approved*.
- If cancellation is approved, the status is set to *cancelled*.

The service task *Set vacation request status to "processing cancellation"*, which is in the flow for handling cancellation of a request that is already approved, changes the request status to indicate that a cancellation is in progress. Follow these steps:

1. Select the task and go to the Details panel, Execution tab, Operations pane.
2. Click Add.
3. In the Select target box, double-click `vacationRequestToCancel`.
4. Click "Takes value of" and then from the Operator type menu choose "Use a Java method."
5. In the list of methods, choose `setStatus`, and then click OK.
6. Click the pencil icon beside the righthand box. This opens the expression editor.
7. In the Expression type list, choose Constant, then in the Value box type **processing cancellation**, and click OK.

Next, update the vacation request status for a request when the manager refuses the cancellation. Select the *Reset vacation request status to approved* service task, then follow the same steps as for the *Set vacation request status to "processing cancellation"* but for this task set the status to *approved*.

Finally, update the vacation request status for a request when the manager approves the cancellation and when a pending request is cancelled. Select the *Update vacation request status* service task, then follow the same steps as for the *Set vacation request status to "processing cancellation"* but for this task set the status to *cancelled*.

Update the number of available vacation days

Update the number of days of vacation that the user has after a successful cancellation. This is done in two service tasks, *Get vacation available*, which gets the current number of available days, and *Credit vacation available*, which updates this total by adding the number of days that were assigned in the cancelled vacation request.

First, configure *Get vacation available*, as follows:

1. Select the task, go to the Details panel, Execution tab, Operations pane, and click Add.
2. In the Select target box, double-click `requesterVacationAvailable`.
3. Leave the operation type set to the default, Takes value of.
4. Click the pencil icon beside the righthand box to open the expression editor.
5. In the Expression type list, choose Query.
6. In the Business Object menu, choose `VacationAvailable`. This automatically sets the Query to `findByBonitaBPMId`. The query definition is displayed.
7. In the Parameters box, the query parameter, `bonitaBPMId`, is listed. You need to specify the value for this, which you do with another expression:

    a. Click in the Value field to activate it, then click the pencil icon at the righthand side.

    b. In the new expression editor, set the Expression type to Java, choose `vacationRequestToCancel` from the Name list, choose `getRequesterBonitaBPMId` from the object tree, and then click OK.

8. The query definition is now complete, so click OK again. You have now defined an operation to retrieve the number of days of vacation available to the user.

Next, configure *Credit vacation available*, as follows:

1. Select the task, go to the Details panel, Execution tab, Operations pane, and click Add.
2. In the Select targe box, double-click `requesterVacationAvailable`.
3. Click "Takes value of" and then from the Operator type menu, choose "Use a Java method."
4. In the list of methods, choose `setDaysAvailableCounter`, and then click OK.
5. Click the pencil icon beside the righthand box. This opens the expression editor.
6. In the Expression type list, choose Script.
7. Set the script name to **resetVacationAvailable**.
8. Enter the following script:

    ```
    requesterVacationAvailable.daysAvailableCounter +
        vacationRequestToCancel.numberOfDays
    ```

9. Check that the Return type is set to `java.lang.Integer`, then click OK to save the definition.

This completes the diagram for the cancellation process.

Update the Tahiti-NewVacationRequest Process

Next, update the *Tahiti-NewVacationRequest* process to receive the cancellation message from the *Tahiti-CancelVacationRequest* process and delete the pending request. Follow these steps:

1. In the *New Vacation Request* pool, select the *reviewRequest* task.
2. In the context menu, click the symbol to add a boundary event.
3. From the list of icons, choose the catch message icon. This adds a catch message boundary event to the *reviewRequest* task.
4. Select the catch message boundary event to display its context menu.
5. Drag the circle icon to create a terminate end event called *end when request cancelled*.
6. Select the catch message boundary event again, and configure it:
   a. Go to the Details panel, General tab, General pane.
   b. Set the event name to **Catch cancellation message** and hide the label (set this in the Appearance tab).
   c. In the Catch message field, specify the name of the message. Do this by typing **cancellationMessage** in the drop-down list.
   d. Go to the Correlation pane and click Add.
   e. In the first column, type **requestId**.
   f. In the second column, click the pencil icon. The expression editor opens.
   g. Set the Expression type to Java.
   h. Select the `vacationRequest` object in the **Name** column, then in the "Browse your Java object" box, click `getPersistenceId()`.
   i. Click OK.

This completes the update to the *New Vacation Request* pool, and in particular to the `reviewRequest` task. When you have finished, this part of the diagram should look something like Figure 11-3:

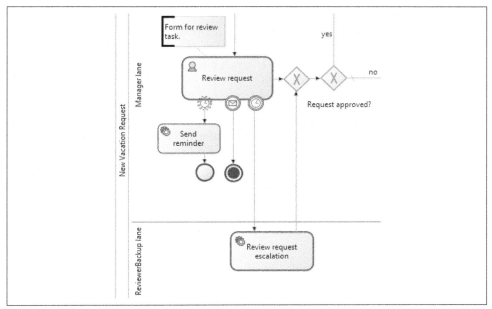

Figure 11-3. The updated reviewRequest task with boundary events

Create Cancellation Process Forms

This process is started by an API call when an employee submits a cancellation request. The request contains all the information that is needed, so there is no instantiation form. To remove the flag warning that no form is defined, select the pool, go to the Details panel, Execution tab, Instantiation form pane, and check No form. You can do the same to remove the warning that no Overview page is defined.

You do need to create the form that the manager will use to review cancellation requests for previously approved vacation requests. This form needs to return the manager's decision to the process, so this is stated in the contract. It also needs to present the manager with the information needed to make the decision; that is, the details of the vacation request and the number of unbooked vacation days that the user has.

To create the contract and the default form, follow these steps:

1. In the *Tahiti-CancelVacationRequest* diagram, select the *Review cancellation* task.
2. Go to the Details panel, Execution tab, Contract pane.
3. Click Add to add an input to the contract.
4. In the Name column, type **cancellationApprovedContract**.
5. Set the type to Boolean.
6. Do not check the box in the Multiple column.

7. Optionally, enter a Description.
8. In the top-right of the **Details** panel, click the UI Designer icon to create the form.
9. When the form opens in the UI Designer, change the name to **cancellationReviewForm**.

The form that is created automatically contains only two widgets: one to capture whether or not the reviewer approves the cancellation, and the other a Submit button. To make the form useful you need to define some variables and add widgets to display information about the user who is requesting the cancellation and about the request that is to be cancelled.

Adding variables to the cancellation review form

This section explains how to add the variables that are necessary for the cancellation review form. Follow these steps:

1. Add an External API variable called `vacationRequestBusinessData` with the API URL `../{{context.vacationRequestToCancel_ref.link}}`. This variable uses the reference to the request to be cancelled that is provided automatically in the context, and retrieves the request details.
2. Add an External API variable called `requester` with the API URL `../API/identity/user/{{vacationRequestBusinessData.requesterBonitaBPMId}}`. This gets the ID of the user requesting the cancellation.
3. Add an External API variable called `requesterCurrentDaysAvailable` with the API URL `../API/bdm/businessData/com.company.model.VacationAvailable?q=findByBonitaBPMId&amp;p=0&amp;c=1&amp;f=bonitaBPMId={{vacationRequestBusinessData.requesterBonitaBPMId}}`. This uses the `requesterBonitaBPMId` from `vacationRequestBusinessData` to get the current number of available days of the requester.

Adding widgets to the cancellation review form

Now you can add widgets to the form to display the information about the user and the request using the variables that you have just defined. Follow these steps:

1. Add a Title widget with a title for the form, *Vacation Cancellation Request*.
2. Add a Text widget containing information to explain the form to the manager. In the Text property, enter the following: *This is a request from {{requester.firstname}} {{requester.lastname}} to cancel a vacation that has already been approved. This employee currently has {{requesterCurrentDaysAvailable}} vacation days available. If you approve this cancellation, this will increase by {{vacationRequestBusinessData.numberOfDays}} days.*
   This text uses the variables that you have defined to present the manager with

information about the user requesting the cancellation, including the number of days of vacation they currently have and would have if the cancellation request is approved.

3. Add a Title widget for this part of the form. Set the Title level to 4 and enter this text: **Details of request to be cancelled:**.

4. Add widgets to present the details of the request that the user wants to cancel. Put the three widgets that display the request details on the same line.

Start date:

Widget type	Datepicker
Width	4
Read-only	yes
Label	Start date
Value	vacationRequestBusinessData.startDate

Return date:

Widget type	Datepicker
Width	4
Read-only	yes
Label	Return date
Value	vacationRequestBusinessData.returnDate

Number of days:

Widget type	Input
Width	4
Read-only	yes
Label	Number of days
Value	vacationRequestBusinessData.numberOfDays

5. Add a Radio buttons widget called Decision for the reviewer to specify whether they approve or refuse the cancellation request. Set the properties as follows:

   a. Set the Available values property to:

```
[{"display":"Approve cancellation", "value": true},
 {"display":"Refuse cancellation", "value":  false}]
```

b. For the Selected value, go to the Decision widget that was created automatically and copy the value from the Value property. Paste this into the Selected value property for the Radio buttons widget.

c. Set the Displayed key property to **display** and Returned key to **value**.

6. Remove the Decision widget that was added automatically, because you have replaced it with the Radio buttons widget.

7. Preview the form and adjust the widget layout if necessary.

You have now created the form that managers will use to review cancellation requests.

Testing Modify and Cancel

To test the processes and updated pages, follow the steps in Chapter 10, but this time deploy all the processes, as well as the new *TahitiVacationManagement* page.

Summary

In this chapter, you have updated the Tahiti application to enable users to modify and cancel vacation requests, and added the process required to handle these changes. You have now created three diagrams, *Tahiti-NewVacationRequest*, *Tahiti-ModifyPendingVacationRequest*, and *Tahiti-CancelVacationRequest*, and downloaded a process to initialize data for testing.

In the next chapter, you will configure service tasks to send email and update calendar events during these processes.

CHAPTER 12

Connecting to Other Systems

In the previous chapter, you created processes to deal with modifying or cancelling a vacation request.

This chapter explains how to add connections from your process to external systems. These connections are not part of the BPMN standard, but most BPM software includes features for exchanging information with external systems. In Bonita BPM, these features are called connectors.

You will use two connectors, one to send email and another to create and manage a calendar entry corresponding to each vacation request.

Email Connectors

When you created the processes, you added several service tasks that send an email message. At each of these tasks, you must configure an email connector with the message header (To, Sender, and Subject) and the message content.

To make the process more flexible, the values that are static for a deployment or that are used in more than one connector can be stored in a parameter. A parameter is declared for a process, and the value is the same each time it is used in the process. Parameters are configured when you prepare a process for deployment, so it is easy to update them. For example, if you use a parameter for the email server address, you can use your local email server for testing during development, but use the company email server in production without changing the process definition, simply by changing the parameter value.

First define the parameters, then define the email connectors, as described in the following sections.

Note that you can save time when configuring a connector by creating a copy of a connector of the same type that is already configured in the same pool. Select the configured connector and click Move/Copy. In the dialog, check the Copy box, then choose the target task where you want to add a connector that is a copy. After you have copied the connector, you can edit it.

Email Connector Parameters

These parameters are used in all the email connectors in the Tahiti processes. You need to set them to the appropriate values for your email server:

- `emailServerAddress`
- `emailServerPassword`
- `emailServerPort`
- `emailServerUsername`
- `emailServerUseSSL`

There is also a parameter, `emailNotificationSender`, that defines the Sender address for email sent from the Tahiti application.

Finally, there is a parameter, `emailHRAddress`, that defines the To address for email sent to HR.

Define each parameter as follows:

1. Select the pool and go to the Details panel, Data tab, Parameters pane.
2. Click Add. The New parameter popup opens.
3. Enter the parameter name.
4. Optionally (but recommended), enter a description.
5. Choose the data type from the Type drop-down menu, choosing the type that matches the connector input type (integer for `emailServerPort`, Boolean for `emailServerUseSSL`, text for the rest).
6. Click "Finish & Add" to add the next parameter, or Finish to exit from the popup.

You need to define these email parameters in both the *Tahiti-NewVacationRequest* and the *Tahiti-CancelVacationRequest* processes.

Now you can configure the email connectors. In some cases, the service task where the connector is defined is already created in the diagram. In others, you need to add the service task first.

Email Connectors in Tahiti-NewVacationRequest

This section explains how to configure the email connectors in the *Tahiti-NewVacationRequest* process.

Notify manager request pending

This connector sends a message to a manager when someone in their team has submitted a vacation request. It informs the manager that there is a pending request to review. The message is sent on behalf of the employee, asking the manager to review the vacation request. Add a service task, *Notify manager request pending*, in the *Employee* lane after the *Deduct requested days from available days* service task.

To define the email connector in the *Notify manager request pending* service task, follow these steps:

1. Select the service task in the whiteboard.
2. Go to the Details panel, Execution tab, Connectors In pane.
3. Click Add. A connector definition wizard opens.
4. In the list of Categories, choose Messaging.
5. In the list of Connector definitions, choose Email, and then click Next.
6. Enter a name for the connector, `emailNotifyManagerRequestPending`.
7. Optionally, enter a description.
8. Specify the behavior if the connector fails by selecting an option from the drop-down menu. If you have an email server and account that you can use for testing, choose "Put in failed state." Otherwise, choose "Ignore error and continue process," so that the process does not wait for the email to be sent. Then click Next.
9. Configure the connection information. This is where you will use the parameters that you have defined:

   - For the Security & SSL field, click "Switch editor to create a condition." Then click the pencil icon, choose Parameters from the Expression type list, and choose `emailServerUseSSL`.
   - For the other fields, click the pencil icon, go to the Parameters list, and choose the relevant parameter:

Field	Parameter
SMTP Host	emailServerAddress
SMTP Port	emailServerPort
Authentication > Username	emailServerUsername
Authentication > Password	emailServerPassword

10. Click Next, which takes you to the screen to configure addressing information.
11. In the From field, choose the parameter `emailNotificationSender`.
12. The To field defines the address to which the email will be sent. This is the manager of the employee who submitted the vacation request. This information

depends on the request, and could change during the lifetime of the application if the organization reporting structure changes, so the value is defined with a script, as follows:

a. Click the pencil icon next to the To field. This opens the expression editor.
b. In the Expression type list, choose Script.
c. Enter the script name, **setReviewerEmailAddress**.
d. Enter this script:

```
import org.bonitasoft.engine.identity.ContactData
import org.bonitasoft.engine.identity.User

User requesterUserInfo =
 BonitaUsers.getUser(apiAccessor,
  vacationRequest.requesterBonitaBPMId)

ContactData managerProfessionalContactInfo =
 BonitaUsers.getUserProfessionalContactInfo(apiAccessor,
  requesterUserInfo.managerUserId)

return managerProfessionalContactInfo.email
```

13. Click OK to save the script and close the expression editor. Then click Next.
14. Enter the email subject: **Vacation request to review**.
15. Enter the message text: **Please go to the Tahiti application and review this pending request from a member of your team.** It is also possible to define the message content with a script and use variables, for example, to include the employee name, but for simplicity here you will use a static message.
16. Click Finish.

The email connector for this service task is now configured. An icon is added to the service task showing that it contains a connector. This part of the *Tahiti-NewVacationRequest* diagram now looks something like Figure 12-1:

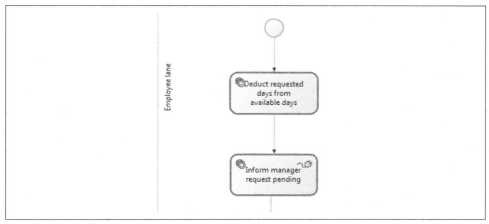

Figure 12-1. Service task for informing manager of a vacation request for review

Send reminder

Configure this connector on the *Send reminder* service task in the *Tahiti-NewVacationRequest* process diagram. It sends a reminder to a manager when a pending request has been waiting for review for more than seven days.

Follow the same steps to configure this email connector (or copy a connector you have already created in the same diagram). This is the specific information for this connector:

- **Name**: *emailRemindManagerRequestPending*
- **To**: Specify a script called *searchReviewerEmailAddress* that returns the To value, with the following content:

```
import org.bonitasoft.engine.identity.ContactData
import org.bonitasoft.engine.identity.User

User requesterUserInfo =
  BonitaUsers.getUser(apiAccessor,
   vacationRequest.bonitaEmployeeId)

ContactData managerProfessionalContactInfo =
  BonitaUsers.getUserProfessionalContactInfo(apiAccessor,
   requesterUserInfo.managerUserId)

return managerProfessionalContactInfo.email
```

- **Subject**: Reminder! You have a vacation request to review waiting for more than 7 days.

- **Message**: Please go to the Tahiti application and review this pending request from a member of your team.

The other information required is the same as for the email connector on the *Inform manager request pending* task.

Notify employee request approved

This connector sends a message to the requester when a vacation request is approved.

Follow the same steps as before (or copy a connector you have already created) to configure this email connector. This is the specific information for this connector:

- **Name**: *emailNotifyEmployeeRequestApproved*
- **To**: Specify a script called *findRequesterEmailAddress* that returns the To value with the following content:

```
return BonitaUsers.getProcessInstanceInitiatorProfessionalContactInfo(
    apiAccessor, processInstanceId).email
```

- **Subject**: Your vacation request has been approved
- **Message**: Enjoy!

Notify employee request refused

This connector sends a message to the requester when a vacation request is refused.

Follow the same steps as before to configure this email connector. This is the specific information for this connector:

- **Name**: *emailNotifyEmployeeRequestRefused*
- **To**: Specify a script called *findRequesterEmailAddress* that returns the To value with the following content (this is the same as for the *Notify employee request accepted* connector):

```
return BonitaUsers.getProcessInstanceInitiatorProfessionalContactInfo(
    apiAccessor, processInstanceId).email
```

- **Subject**: Your vacation request has been refused
- **Message**: Sorry. See your manager for the reason why this request has been refused.

Notify HR request refused

This connector sends a message to the HR team when a vacation request is refused.

Follow the same steps as before to configure this email connector. This is the specific information for this connector:

- **Name:** *emailNotifyHRRequestRefused*
- **To:** Specify the parameter *emailHRAddress*
- **Subject:** Vacation refusal
- **Message:** Specify this with a script called *vacationRefusalDetails*. To do this, click Switch editor to create a condition, then click the pencil icon and specify a script with the following content:

```
import java.text.SimpleDateFormat

import org.bonitasoft.engine.api.IdentityAPI
import org.bonitasoft.engine.identity.User

// Create a date formatter that will format the date stored in
// business data to a user readable format
SimpleDateFormat formatter = new SimpleDateFormat("MM-dd-yyyy",
 Locale.US)
formatter.timezone = TimeZone.getTimeZone("UTC")

// Get a reference to IdentityAPI in order to retrieve user
// information using user id
IdentityAPI identityAPI = apiAccessor.identityAPI

// Requester user information
User requester = identityAPI.getUser(
 vacationRequest.requesterBonitaBPMId)

// Reviewer user information
User reviewer = identityAPI.getUser(
 vacationRequest.reviewerBonitaBPMId)

return "The vacation request submitted by \
 ${requester.getFirstName()} ${requester.getLastName()} \
 for ${formatter.format(vacationRequest.getStartDate())} to \
 ${formatter.format(vacationRequest.getReturnDate())} \
 (${vacationRequest.getNumberOfDays()} days) \
 has been rejected by ${reviewer.getFirstName()} \
 ${reviewer.getLastName()} \
 with the following comment: ${vacationRequest.getComments()}"
```

Email Connectors in Tahiti-CancelVacationRequest

This section explains how to configure the email connectors in the *Tahiti-CancelVacationRequest* process. First add these service tasks for the connectors:

- *Notify manager cancellation request to review* in the *Employee lane* after the *Set vacation request status to "processing cancellation"* service task

- *Notify employee cancellation approved* in the *Manager lane* on the *Yes* flow out of the *Cancellation approved?* gateway
- *Notify employee cancellation refused* in the *Manager lane* on the *No* flow out of the *Cancellation approved?* gateway

When you have added these service tasks, this part of the diagram will look something like Figure 12-2:

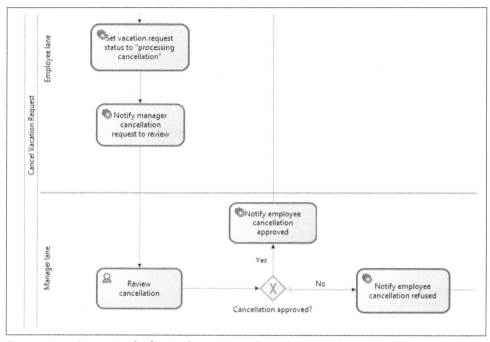

Figure 12-2. Service tasks for sending an email notification when cancelling a vacation request

Notify manager cancellation request to review

This connector sends a message to a manager when someone in their team has submitted a request to cancel a vacation request that is already approved. It informs the manager that there is a cancellation request to review.

Follow the steps in the previous section to configure the connector (including parameters declaration in the pool). This is the specific information for this connector:

- **Name**: *emailNotifyManagerCancellationToReview*
- **To**: Specify a script called *searchReviewerEmailAddress* that returns the To value with the following content:

```
import org.bonitasoft.engine.identity.ContactData
import org.bonitasoft.engine.identity.User

User requesterUserInfo =
 BonitaUsers.getUser(apiAccessor,
  vacationRequest.bonitaEmployeeId)

ContactData managerProfessionalContactInfo =
 BonitaUsers.getUserProfessionalContactInfo(apiAccessor,
  requesterUserInfo.managerUserId)

return managerProfessionalContactInfo.email
```

- **Subject**: Vacation cancellation request to review
- **Message**: Please go to the Tahiti application and review this cancellation request from a member of your team.

The other information required is the same as for the email connector on the *Inform manager request pending* task.

Notify employee cancellation approved

This connector sends a message to the requester when a vacation cancellation request is approved.

Follow the same steps as before (or copy a connector you have already created in this diagram) to configure this email connector. This is the specific information for this connector:

- **Name**: *emailNotifyEmployeeCancellationApproved*
- **To**: Specify a script called *findRequesterEmailAddress* that returns the To value with the following content:

```
return BonitaUsers.getProcessInstanceInitiatorProfessionalContactInfo(
 apiAccessor, processInstanceId).email
```

- **Subject**: Your vacation cancellation request has been approved
- **Message**: Your manager has approved your vacation cancellation request.

Notify employee cancellation refused

This connector sends a message to the requester when a vacation cancellation request is refused.

Follow the same steps as before (or copy the *emailNotifyEmployeeCancellationApproved* connector you have already created in this diagram) to configure this email connector. This is the specific information for this connector:

- **Name**: *emailNotifyEmployeeCancellationRefused*
- **To**: Specify a script called *findRequesterEmailAddress* that returns the To value with the following content:

```
return BonitaUsers.getProcessInstanceInitiatorProfessionalContactInfo(
  apiAccessor, processInstanceId).email
```

- **Subject**: Your vacation cancellation request has been refused
- **Message**: Your manager has refused your vacation cancellation request. Please discuss this with your manager.

Calendar Connectors

Calendar connectors manage entries in a Google calendar. There are connectors for each type of interaction with the calendar. You have not yet added the service tasks that update the calendar, so in the following sections you need to add the task and then configure the connector.

The processes in the Tahiti application create, update, and delete calendar events, as follows:

- When a vacation request is submitted, a calendar event is created showing the employee name and the vacation request status: pending.
- When a request is modified, the corresponding calendar event is updated.
- When a request is approved, the corresponding event is updated to change the status from pending to approved.
- When a request is rejected by the manager or cancelled by the employee, the corresponding calendar event is removed.

The calendar connector uses Google Data API feeds. Before you can use the connector, you need to create a Google Apps service account and get connection credentials. This can either be a paid account or a time-limited trial account. You then need to configure the calendar client to authorize access to calendar events in your Google domain. See the Bonita BPM documentation (*http://bit.ly/bonita-gcal*) for details of how to create a service account and configure the client. When you create the service account, be sure to note the Client ID and Email address from the Credentials page, and to keep a copy of the private key *.p12* file.

Calendar Connector Parameters

Use parameters to make it easier to configure the calendar connectors, to avoid repeating information, and to make it easier to update settings later. Define the following parameters:

calendarApplicationName

A unique name used to identify the calling application. For example, TahitiVacationManagement.

calendarCalendarId

The email address that identifies the calendar to be accessed. For example, acme.com_g54gxf547fx564f6@group.calendar.google.com.

calendarServiceAccountId

The email address of the Google client that you noted when you created the service account. For example, 012345678901-g454gcfxj4jb5@developer.gserviceaccount.com.

calendarServiceAccountP12File

The full path to the private key file that you saved when you created the service account. For example, C:/my/folder/path/tahitiApps-54vhc5fgh1.p12.

calendarServiceAccountUser

The email address of the user accessing the calendar. This account must have appropriate rights to modify the calendar. You could use the calendar owner, for example, tahiti.vacationmanagement@acme.com.

You need to define these calendar parameters in the *Tahiti-newVacationRequest*, *Tahiti-ModifyPendingVacationRequest*, and *Tahiti-CancelVacationRequest* processes.

Date Formatter Groovy Script

Google Calendar APIs require a specific date format: *yyyy-MM-dd*.

This means that you need to convert between the format used in the business data and the one required by the Google Calendar APIs. The conversion needs to happen when providing start and end dates in the Calendar connectors.

We will use a Groovy script to define this format conversion. The same conversion is needed each time we configure a Calendar connector, so we will define a Groovy script that can be used by all processes defined in the workspace:

1. Go to the Development menu, Manage Groovy scripts... menu entry.
2. Click Create.
3. Enter a name for the new script, **DateTimeScripts**, and click OK.
4. In the list, select the newly created script and then click Open.
5. Enter the following script content:

```
public static String formatForGoogle(Date date) {
  // Create a date formatter that will format the date stored
  // in business data to the format expected by
  // Google Calendar API
  java.text.SimpleDateFormat formatter =
```

```
        new java.text.SimpleDateFormat("yyyy-MM-dd", Locale.US)

        formatter.timeZone = TimeZone.getTimeZone("UTC")

        // Returns the formatted date
        return formatter.format(date)
    }
```

6. Click OK to save the script definition, and then click Cancel to close the popup window.

Update calendar request pending

After an employee submits a vacation request, there needs to be a service task that creates a vacation calendar entry, so that the request is visible to the whole team. In the *Tahiti-NewVacationRequest* diagram, add a service task called *Update calendar request pending*. Your diagram will look something like Figure 12-3.

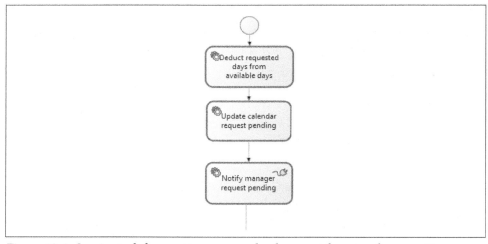

Figure 12-3. Service task for creating a new calendar event for a pending vacation request

To configure the calendar connector, follow these steps:

1. Select the *Update calendar request pending* task, and go to the Details panel, Execution tab, Connectors in pane.
2. Click Add. This opens the connector configuration wizard.
3. In the Categories list, expand the Calendar category and choose Google Calendar (API v3).
4. In the Connector definitions list, choose Create Event, and then click Next.
5. Enter a name for this connector, **calRegisterVacationEvent**.

6. Set the failure behavior to "Ignore error and continue process," and then click Next.
7. Configure the connection information. This is where you will use the parameters that you have defined. For each field, click the arrow to open the drop-down list and choose the relevant parameter:

Field	Parameter
Application name	calendarApplicationName
Calendar ID	calendarCalendarId
Service Account ID	calendarServiceAccountId
Service Account P12 file	calendarServiceAccountP12File
Service Account User	calendarServiceAccountUser

8. Click Next to go to the event parameters screen. Enter the following information:

   a. Summary: The title of the event that is displayed in the calendar. Specify this as a Groovy script called *Requester first name and last name + pending status*, with the following content:

```
import org.bonitasoft.engine.api.IdentityAPI
import org.bonitasoft.engine.identity.User

// Get reference to IdentityAPI to access user's first and
// last name using the user id stored in the VacationRequest
IdentityAPI identityAPI = apiAccessor.identityAPI

// Retrieve user information using the API and user id stored
// in business data
User user = identityAPI.getUser(
 vacationRequest.requesterBonitaBPMId)

// Aggregate user first and last name and return the result
return user.firstName + " " + user.lastName + " " +
 vacationRequest.status
```

   b. Start Date: The first date of the requested vacation. Specify this as a Groovy script called *format start date*, with the following content:

```
DateTimeScripts.formatForGoogle(vacationRequest.startDate)
```

   c. Start Time Timezone: Set this to UTC (you can type the value in the field).
   d. Check the box for All Day.
   e. End Date: The return to work day (because a Google Calendar end date is exclusive). Specify this as a Groovy script called *format return date*, with the following content:

```
DateTimeScripts.formatForGoogle(vacationRequest.returnDate)
```

f. End Time Timezone: Set this to UTC.

g. Click Next.

9. In the Extra Event Parameters screen, specify the Attendee, as follows:

a. Click Add row.

b. Click in the empty new row. The pencil icon appears.

c. Click the pencil icon to open the expression editor.

d. Create a script expression called *return requester email address* with the following content:

```
import org.bonitasoft.engine.identity.ContactData

Long userId = vacationRequest.requesterBonitaBPMId

ContactData professionalContactInfo =
  BonitaUsers.getUserProfessionalContactInfo(apiAccessor, userId)

return professionalContactInfo.email
```

10. Click Next twice to get to the Output operations screen.

11. In the Output operations screen, define an operation to store the calendar event ID in the vacation request, as follows:

a. In the Select target drop-down menu, double-click *vacationRequest*.

b. Click "Takes value of." This opens the Select operator popup.

c. In the popup, select "Use a Java method." This opens a list of methods.

d. Choose **setCalendarEventId** from the list and click OK.

e. Click the pencil icon next to the right field. This opens the expression editor.

f. Set the Expression type to Connector output.

g. In the list of outputs, choose ID, and then click OK.

h. Optionally you can remove default output operations: for each operation click the button with the red cross icon.

12. Click Finish.

Update calendar request modified

If a user modifies a vacation request, the associated calendar event needs to be updated. In the *Tahiti-ModifyPendingRequest* diagram, add the service task *Update calendar* to update the calendar event with the new dates. Your diagram will look something like Figure 12-4.

Figure 12-4. Service task for updating the calendar for a modified vacation request

Configure a calendar connector on this service task to modify the calendar event. Follow the same steps as for the "Update calendar request pending" on page 124, with the following differences:

- Connector definition: Update Event.
- Name: *calUpdateEventDetails*.
- Event ID: The ID of the calendar event, specified as follows:

  1. Beside the Event ID field, click the pencil icon to open the expression editor.
  2. In the Expression type list, choose Java.
  3. In the Name list, choose `vacationRequest`.
  4. In the browse box, choose `getCalendarEventId()`.
  5. Click OK.

- Start Date: The new start date for the vacation request, specified as follows:

  1. Beside the Start Date field, click the pencil icon to open the expression editor.
  2. In the Expression type list, choose Script.
  3. In the Name field, type **formatStartDate**.
  4. Enter the following script:

     ```
     DateTimeScripts.formatForGoogle(vacationRequest.startDate)
     ```

  5. Click OK to close the expression editor.
  6. Start Time Timezone: Set this to UTC (you can type the value in the field).
  7. Check the box for All Day.

- End Date: The new end date for the vacation request, specified as follows:

  1. Beside the End Date field, click the pencil icon to open the expression editor.
  2. In the Expression type list, choose Script.
  3. In the Name field, type **formatReturnDate**.
  4. Enter the following script:

     ```
     DateTimeScripts.formatForGoogle(vacationRequest.returnDate)
     ```

  5. Click OK to close the expression editor.
  6. Ent Time Timezone: Set this to UTC (you can type the value in the field).

Update calendar approved

When a manager approves a vacation request, the associated calendar event needs to be updated to show that the request is no longer pending but is approved. In the *Tahiti-NewVacationRequest* diagram, add a service task called *Update calendar request approved* on the *yes* flow from the *Request approved?* gateway (see Figure 12-5).

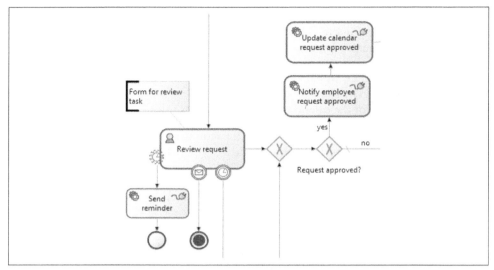

Figure 12-5. Service task for updating the calendar for an approved vacation request

On this service task, configure a calendar connector to update the calendar event to change the status from pending to approved.

Follow the same steps as for the "Update calendar request pending" on page 124, with the following differences:

- Connector definition: Update Event
- Name: *calUpdateVacationEventName.*
- Event ID: The ID of the calendar event, specified as follows:

  1. Beside the Event ID field, click the pencil icon to open the expression editor.
  2. In the Expression type list, choose Java.
  3. In the Name list, choose vacationRequest.
  4. In the browse box, choose getCalendarEventId().
  5. Click OK.

- Summary: The updated event title. Specify this as a Groovy script called *new status approved*, with the following content:

```
import org.bonitasoft.engine.api.IdentityAPI
import org.bonitasoft.engine.identity.User

// Get reference to IdentityAPI to access user's first and last
// name using the user id stored in the VacationRequest
IdentityAPI identityAPI = apiAccessor.identityAPI

// Retrieve user information using the API and user id stored in
// business data
```

```
User user = identityAPI.getUser(
  vacationRequest.requesterBonitaBPMId)

// Aggregate user first and last name and return the result
return user.firstName + " " + user.lastName + " " +
  vacationRequest.status
```

- You do not need to specify the attendee or an output operation. You do not need to specify the vacation request details such as the start date, because these have not changed.

Update calendar request refused

When a manager refuses a vacation request, the associated calendar event needs to be removed from the calendar. In the *Tahiti-NewVacationRequest* diagram, add a service task called *Update calendar request refused* on the *no* flow from the *Request approved?* gateway (see Figure 12-6).

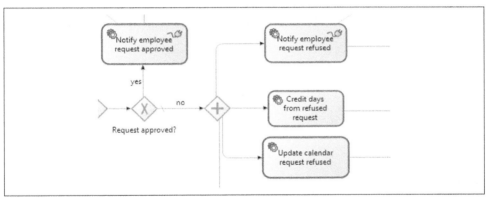

Figure 12-6. Service task for removing a refused request from the calendar

Configure a calendar Delete event connector called *calRemoveRefusedVacationEvent*. Define the Event ID as in the previous section.

Update calendar request cancelled

If a vacation request is cancelled, it must be removed from the calendar. In the *Tahiti-CancelVacationRequest* process diagram, add a service task called *Update calendar request cancelled* before the gateway at the end of the flow handling a successful cancellation (see Figure 12-7).

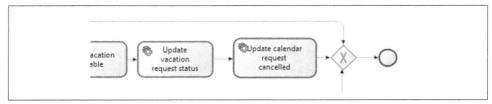

Figure 12-7. Service task for removing a cancelled request from the calendar

Configure a Delete event connector called *calRemoveCancelledVacationEvent*. Define the Event ID as in the previous section using the `vacationRequestToCancel` object.

Summary

You have updated the diagram to specify the email and calendar connectors required in the *New Vacation Request* process. The services tasks with connectors now display the connector icon.

The next chapter describes how to create the complete version of the Tahiti vacation management application.

CHAPTER 13

Finishing the Application

In the previous chapter, you completed the process definitions by adding connectors to send email and to manage calendar events. You have now created all the processes, forms, connectors, and pages used in the Tahiti application.

In this chapter, you will update the forms used in the Tahiti application processes so that the application page is displayed after a form is submitted. Next, you will update the application to include the final page. Finally, you will deploy the processes.

When you have updated the Tahiti application and deployed its processes, you will validate it in the development environment using a scenario that checks all the usage paths.

Updating Process Forms

In this section, you will update the process forms so that after the user clicks Submit on a form, the Tahiti application page is displayed. If you do not do this, after a form is submitted the default page is displayed. This is the user's task list in the Bonita BPM Portal. If the users do not use the Portal for other processes, displaying this page could be confusing, so it is better to specify a page.

First, you need to get the URL of the Tahiti application that you defined in the Portal:

1. Log in to Bonita BPM Portal and set the Profile to Administrator.
2. Go to Applications. A list of the applications that you have defined is displayed, including a partial URL for each one.
3. Find the Tahiti application that you defined in "Create the Application Prototype" on page 15 and click the URL. If you followed the suggestion, the URL is `http://localhost:8080/bonita/apps/tahiti/index/` (adjust 8080 to the port used by your running Studio).

4. We suggest you don't include the host name ("localhost" in this example) in your form properties because it will change based on the server where you will deploy your application. Instead, use a relative URL: `/bonita/apps/tahiti/index/`. Save this URL to add to the forms.

Now that you have the URL, you can update the forms. There are three forms to update, *newVacationRequestForm*, *reviewRequestForm*, and *cancellationReviewForm*. For the *newVacationRequestForm*, follow these steps:

1. In Bonita BPM Studio, open the *Tahiti-NewVacationRequest* process diagram.
2. Select the pool, and then go to the Details panel, Execution tab, Instantiation form pane.
3. Find the Target form field, which shows the name of the form, *newVacationRequestForm*. Click the pencil icon beside this field. This opens the UI Designer with the form displayed.
4. Select the Submit button widget and go to the Properties panel.
5. Set the value of the "Target URL on success" property to the URL that you saved earlier.
6. Click Save at the top of the UI Designer to save the form, and then close it.

Now go back to the process diagram and select the *Review request* human task. Follow the same steps to open and update the *reviewRequestForm* form. For *cancellationReviewForm*, open the *Tahiti-CancelVacationRequest* process, go to the *Review cancellation* task, and update the form.

Update the Application

In "Add a Cancel Option to the Application Page" on page 100 you created the final version of the Tahiti application home page, which you exported as a *.zip* archive. All you need to do to update the application is replace the previous page with this final version. Follow these steps:

1. Log in to the Bonita BPM Portal, and switch to the Administrator profile.
2. Go to the **Resources** screen.
3. In the list of Pages, select *TahitiVacationManagement*, and then click **Edit**.
4. In the popup, specify the *page-TahitiVacationManagement.zip* file that you exported earlier, and then click **Next**.
5. In the confirmation popup, click **Confirm**. The page will be imported.
6. Go to the **Applications** screen.
7. Click the URL to view the Tahiti application page and check that the correct page is displayed.
8. Bookmark the URL of the page to make it easier to test the application later in this chapter.

You have now completed the updates to the Tahiti application.

Deploy the Processes

You have updated the application to use the updated page. Next, you need to deploy the processes that are called by the application:

- *Tahiti-InitiateVacationAvailable*
- *Tahiti-NewVacationRequest*
- *Tahiti-ModifyPendingVacationRequest*
- *Tahiti-CancelVacationRequest*

To do this, go the Bonita BPM Studio. Open each process diagram in turn and click Run in the top menu bar. If you are running a process for the first time since you updated it, there might be some configuration information that you need to provide, and this will be listed in an information message. You can check the configuration is complete manually before running a process, but it is usually quicker to rely on the Studio to check and report any problems.

For the *Tahiti-InitiateVacationAvailable* process, click the button in the displayed form so that the process runs to its conclusion. For the other processes, simply close the browser window where the form or the Portal is displayed. This deploys the process without running it.

The next section explains how to test the Tahiti application in your development environment.

Test the Application

In the previous section, you deployed the Tahiti vacation management application and its processes in your development environment. You have done some testing along the way to make sure that the individual components work, but now it's time to test the whole application. This section outlines a test scenario that will validate almost every aspect of the application and the processes it contains.

There are three users in this scenario:

- Helen Kelly (helen.kelly), the Human Resources manager
- April Sanchez (april.sanchez), a compensation specialist who reports to Helen
- Walter Bates (walter.bates), an HR benefits specialist who also reports to Helen

April and Walter are not managers. All three users have the same password, bpm.

In this scenario, you need to use the Tahiti application as each user in turn, so you log in and log out several times using the Bonita BPM Portal. In a production system, you would probably access the application from your corporate intranet, which would handle the login, and you would not use the Bonita BPM Portal.

The three users log in to the Portal with the User profile, and then access the Tahiti application using the browser bookmark that you created earlier. Each user has 10 days of vacation available. To simplify checking, create all vacation requests for 1 day.

Follow these steps:

1. Log in as Walter and then:
   a. Create two vacation requests.
   b. Select one of these requests and cancel it.
2. Log in as April and then:
   a. Create two vacation requests.
   b. Select one of these requests and modify it to be 2 days.
3. Log in as Helen and then:
   a. Create a vacation request.
   b. View the list of pending requests from the team.
   c. Select the 1-day request from April and refuse it, giving a reason.
   d. Select Walter's pending request and approve it.
4. Log in as Walter and cancel the approved request.

At the end of these steps, Helen's vacation statement should show that she has 9 days available with one pending request, April has 8 days available with one pending request, and Walter has 9 and an outstanding cancellation request.

Summary

You have created the Tahiti vacation management application and validated that it works correctly in the development environment.

The next chapter contains some suggestions about how to test the application in a pre-production environment and prepare it for deployment. It also contains some suggestions to think about for future improvements to the application.

CHAPTER 14

Deploying the Application

In the previous chapter, you created the Tahiti application and ran it in your development environment to validate all the actions presented in the application page and the associated processes. This chapter contains some advice about how to test your application more thoroughly before putting it into production, and explains some of the considerations for setting up the environment required to support the application. Finally, it suggests some ideas for improving the application in future versions.

Testing

When you use a BPM solution to build a process-based application, you need to plan for testing, just like in any other software development process. The details of what testing is required and how you run the tests will depend on your corporate infrastructure and guidelines for acceptance testing to demonstrate that the application is acceptable to be installed.

Typically, testing is done at various levels such as *unit test*, *workflow execution*, and *user acceptance testing*.

Unit Test

Unit tests focus on the source code you write for your processes implementation, addressing each code unit separately.

When you use Bonita BPM, you typically write source code for the following artifacts:

- Java code for connectors, actor filters, event handlers, or libraries included in process definitions. In the Tahiti application, you have not created any Java code.

- Groovy scripts for REST API extensions and in various places in process definitions. In the Tahiti application, you use a REST API extension and many Groovy scripts.
- JavaScript scripts in forms, pages, and custom widgets. In the Tahiti application, you have used many JavaScript scripts in forms and the application page.

Define unit tests in the development environment you use to write the different pieces of source code. If source code is called only in a process definition, you might want to externalize it to make testing easier.

You can usually benefit from the testing tools already used in your development environment. For example, to test Java source code we recommend JUnit (*http://junit.org/*), Mockito (*http://mockito.org/*), and AssertJ (*http://joel-costigliola.github.io/assertj/*).

Workflow Execution

Workflow execution is an integrated test of all the process elements used to execute a usage scenario. This validates the behavior of the processes end to end. In earlier chapters of this book, you have checked the end-to-end workflow using test scenarios that start in the Tahiti application page and then progress through process steps.

As well as test scenarios that execute the happy path of expected user interactions, you should also test all possible branches of each process.

Tests should verify process execution progress by checking which steps are pending, and the process state after giving an order, such as creating a process instance or execution of a step. Tests should also perform checks on the business data to validate consistency with process execution progress. For example, you need a test that verifies that the leave request status is consistent with the user actions taken.

If your process definition is integrated with external systems such as an email server or web services, you need to create mock-ups of the application interactions with these systems. This enables you to test your application and its processes in isolation, without also testing the external systems.

User Acceptance Testing

Unit tests and workflow execution tests primarily cover process definitions with the goal of ensuring that process execution is flawless. For a fully automated process this is all that is required. However, for a process or application that includes user interaction, you also need to test the user interface elements.

Web user interface testing can be automated with tools like Protractor. Such tools are invaluable, though the upfront investment to create test definitions can be high. Also, automated user interface tests do not provide feedback about your application usability.

We recommend that you partially automate this testing, but counterbalance the automated testing with testing done by a panel of users. This way you will quickly catch obvious bugs and gather information for future improvements.

Setting Up the Environment

After you have completed the testing, there are three steps to complete before you can put the Tahiti application into production:

- Set up a Bonita BPM production platform.
- Integrate Bonita BPM and the Tahiti application into your corporate systems. For example, if you manage users with an LDAP system, synchronize this with the Bonita BPM organization. If you have a single sign-on system, extend this to Bonita BPM to grant access to the Tahiti application. The Bonita BPM documentation explains how to do this.
- Create a process for initializing the vacation days available at the start of the vacation year, and for any new hires during the year. The downloadable initialization process is really provided for testing, but you could adapt it to update the available days for all employees at the start of each vacation year.

Future Enhancements

Throughout this book you have been developing the process-based Tahiti vacation management application. You now have a working application that, with a little configuration, you can deploy in your company. But you have probably noticed that there are some things that the application does not do. We made some deliberate decisions to ignore some potential features, either to to avoid duplication, to avoid distracting detail that is not specifically about BPM application, or just for simplicity.

Application development is always iterative, and it's completely normal that you finish the development of version 1 with a list of features for version 2! Here is our list of things that we decided not to cover in this first version of the Tahiti application:

- Handle multiple types of vacation (for example, unpaid vacation, personal days, recoup).
- Handle half days.
- Calculate number of days out or return date instead of asking user to enter them both. Would need logic with knowledge of each employee's work pattern (for example, if part-time) and public/company holidays for each location.

- Monitor unbooked vacation totals automatically and flag potential issues to manager. Would need to compare days unbooked with remaining bookable days, and with some indication of "typical" pattern. For now, we just show the data and expect the manager to draw conclusions.
- Manage the potential concurrent access if user modifies or cancels a pending request while it is being reviewed by the manager. Transaction model means risk is low.
- Permit modification of an approved request.
- Send a notification to the escalation reviewers group when a vacation request review is late.
- Present cancellation requests for review in the manager's Tahiti application page. The manager can use the Bonita BPM Portal to do these tasks.
- Add an escalation path for cancellation requests.
- Present escalated review requests in the Tahiti application page. The users in the escalation group can use the Bonita BPM Portal to do these tasks.
- Handle tables when there is no data to display by showing a message instead of an empty table, so that it is clear this is not an error.
- Add an application page for updating an employee's available vacation or for initializing this for a specific user partway through the year (the new hire case). Keep script for bulk initialization at start of year, but update it to allow for different numbers of days for employees with nonstandard work patterns.
- Support administrative tasks including reporting vacation to payroll.
- Add metrics to track the efficiency of the process. For example, you could track the average time between submission and review for a request for each manager, and how often requests are escalated.

You can add you own ideas here, and then start developing Tahiti2!

Next Steps

Congratulations on staying the course! You have made it to the end of the last chapter of your journey to develop your vacation management application. You can deploy it and get feedback from your employees, and enjoy the efficiency gains over your old manual process.

But this is just your first business process application. Now that you understand how to go about creating a process-based application, take a look at the other business processes in your company: there will be many more processes that you could automate, with even more productivity gains and cost savings.

Index

event-based gateways, 69
exceptions
    defined, 77
    handling, 82
exclusive gateways, 69

F
fail-safe conditions, 77
filtering, 42
findByPersistenceId, 97
findCancellableByBonitaBPMId, 52
findModifiableByBonitaBPMId, 51
flow conditions, managing, 73
forms
    cancellation process, 109
    creating process forms, 63-68
    defined, 63
    manager review, 65-68
    process, 131
    temporary, 57
    vacation modification, 34
    vacation request, 34, 63-65
    vacation request review, 35

G
gateways
    best practices, 70
    exclusive, 69
    inclusive, 70
    overview of, 69
    parallel, 70
    types of, 69
Google Data API, 122
Groovy script (date formatter), 123

H
home page, 36
human tasks
    assigning actors to, 46
    creating, 28
    updating, 37

I
inclusive gateways, 70
indexes, 52
Input widgets, 19
interrupting timers, 79
interruptions

canceling requests, 99-112
    defined, 93
    modifying requests, 93-99
    testing modify and cancel, 112
isManager, 22

J
Java objects
    adding indexes for, 52
    concept of, 47
    defining, 49
    defining queries for, 51
joins, 69
JSON objects, 22
JSON variables, 17
JUnit, 136

L
lanes, 41
Link widgets, 19
login, 36

M
management information
    adding lanes for, 43
    managing decisions, 69-76
    reminders, 77
    team vacation statement, 35
    vacation request review form, 65-68
    vacation statement extensions, 7, 36
managerTeamInfo, 21
mapping, 42
Mockito, 136
modify option, 94
myVacation, 17
myVacationAvailable, 17
myVacationAvailableNumber, 19

N
New Diagram icon (BPM Studio), 27
newRequest variables, 58
noninterrupting boundary timer events, 78
notification tasks, 38
numberOfDays variable, 97

O
OR decisions, 69
organization data, 62

About the Authors

A skilled technical author specializing in leading-edge software, **Christine McKinty** was with Bonitasoft from 2012 to 2015, writing about business process management. Prior to that, she worked as technical writer and user-centered design specialist in the UK and France for international businesses and as an independent consultant. She is based near Grenoble, France. Her passions are people, technology, people using technology, and singing.

Antoine Mottier is a seasoned BPM consultant with Bonitasoft. Over his six years at Bonitasoft, he has played different roles: BPM solutions consultant, training manager, and more recently, technical evangelist. With his technical expertise, he has helped many companies implement successful BPM projects across a wide range of industries such as telecommunications, automotive, banking, insurance, and more.

As a technical evangelist, he is responsible for promoting easy user adoption of the product. He is involved in sharing best practices with analysts and online communities and is also a regular speaker at events and webinars.

Antoine lives in Grenoble, France, and spends his free time in the surrounding mountains, biking, climbing, or skiing.

Colophon

The cover illustration is by Anton Khodakovsky. The cover fonts are DIN and Guardian Sans. The text font is Adobe Minion Pro; the heading font is Adobe Myriad Condensed; and the code font is Dalton Maag's Ubuntu Mono.

Get even more for your money.

Join the O'Reilly Community, and register the O'Reilly books you own. It's free, and you'll get:

- $4.99 ebook upgrade offer
- 40% upgrade offer on O'Reilly print books
- Membership discounts on books and events
- Free lifetime updates to ebooks and videos
- Multiple ebook formats, DRM FREE
- Participation in the O'Reilly community
- Newsletters
- Account management
- 100% Satisfaction Guarantee

Signing up is easy:

1. Go to: oreilly.com/go/register
2. Create an O'Reilly login.
3. Provide your address.
4. Register your books.

Note: English-language books only

To order books online:
oreilly.com/store

For questions about products or an order:
orders@oreilly.com

To sign up to get topic-specific email announcements and/or news about upcoming books, conferences, special offers, and new technologies:
elists@oreilly.com

For technical questions about book content:
booktech@oreilly.com

To submit new book proposals to our editors:
proposals@oreilly.com

O'Reilly books are available in multiple DRM-free ebook formats. For more information:
oreilly.com/ebooks

Lightning Source UK Ltd.
Milton Keynes UK
UKOW05f1238140316

270160UK00002B/2/P